MW01045510

I Want What She's Having

- Naomi Simson

"The experience of creating a
pleasurable business."

First Published 2007

Messenger Publishing
PO Box H241 Australia Square NSW 1215
www.messengermarketing.com.au

**National Library of Australia
Cataloguing-in-Publication Data:**

Simson, Naomi
  I Want What She's Having:
  The Experience of Creating a Pleasurable Business

  1st ed.
  ISBN 9 7809803284 0 0

  1. Simson, Naomi. 2. Businesswomen - Australia -
  Biography. 3. Home-based businesses - Australia.
  4. Performance awards - Australia. I. Title.

Project managed by Messenger Marketing,
www.messengermarketing.com.au

Cover Photography: Peter Collie

Design: Robert Bates, Messenger Marketing

Printed in China through Bookbuilders

Contents

Acknowledgements

This book is an acknowledgement of other peoples' contributions, but I do want to make special mention of a few people.

To the RedBallooners – past, present and future. A special note of thanks to the 'originals' Kirsten Munachen, Jemma Fastnedge and Renee Walliker. However without all of the team, those who make the difference every day, we would not get to do what we do. Thanks team – it is a privilege to work with you.

To my mentors, coaches and buddies – past, present and future. Sarah Hatcher and Diana Ryall – who have supported me in both of my working lives. To Peter Simson, Dominique Lyone and David Cunningham – great business people who have shared their experiences with me. To Cath Pritchard and Janine Peckham who keep me playing a bigger game. And of course to the wonderful Verne Harnish whose work we have put into practice.

To my fellow entrepreneurs – James Stevens, Emma Brown, Narelle Anderson, Andrew Tucker, Adrian Giles, Ben Ridler and the many other members of the Entrepreneurs Organisation.

To my family and friends – Natalia and Oscar, Lorna and Doug Elms, Dwin Tucker, Nigel and Louise Watts, Alison Payne, Margie Hartley and Andrea Pert – because you all believe in me. Thank you for your endless love and support.

A special thanks to Jemma Fastnedge and Sally Kavanagh for their tireless support of me during the writing of this book and their insightful comments and contribution.

An Everyday Woman

I write this book for the woman who said to me after one of my speaking engagements, "I want what you're on!" I don't know your name or where you are from, but your comment got me thinking.

At first I thought indignantly, "I'm not on anything, I'm just being me." Then after much consideration I began to ask, "Am I different or just the same?" I think I am very much the same, not particularly special, or audacious (not even that clever really).

So as a very ordinary person I write of an ordinary journey, but also of the things that I've discovered along the way, that have helped me create an extraordinary business from what began as an experiment.

I truly believe that life is the sum of your experiences. I know that without all the people that I've met, all of the bosses that I have had and friends that I've made I would never have done the things I've done.

This is not particularly my story. Rather, it is the journey of my discoveries, of the things I wish I had known before starting my own show. There are secrets that were discovered from trial and error, there are strategies that have been developed from hundreds of conversations, and there are stories that continue to be re-told. This book comes from my experiences, from things I've learned, things that others have generously shared with me. Keep in mind that this is how I remember the experiences and it is my view of the world.

People often ask me if I will mentor them and I put it on the table – I will willingly share my experiences but I don't put myself in the position of advice because I am not qualified. I don't know their life circumstances.

I learn so much from the many people I meet, and what I learn I then try to pass on to others. It's also why I write my blog, naomisimson.com. This book is about passing on information and being generous by sharing what I've learnt along the way:

- Your past experiences are valuable. Extract what you've learned to help you now.
- View every 'NO' as an opportunity; find an alternative way to achieve it.
- Establish a good open communication system so you can really listen to your customers. Inspire people to 'tell the story' of your business by amazing and delighting them, delivering consistently on your promise and ensuring integrity is present in all your dealings.
- Work out a purpose, not only for yourself but also for your business. Then create a set of values to keep everyone on track daily and aligned with the purpose. I've found that empowering all employees to be leaders helps encourage responsibility.
- Business is just a game, and it's ok to inject fun into your day. People who are happy at work will look after your customers. Happy and loyal customers will bring in great profits for your business. It's not rocket science.
- Make full use of the technology that is available to you – it will save you time, keep you competitive and allow you to serve your customers more effectively.
- Recognize the contribution of your employees and others that provide you with service. It's vital to reverse the high levels of employee disengagement that are harming so many businesses and, in turn, the economy as a whole.

One of my great passions now is the vision and belief that, through RedBalloon, we can change the nature of gifting in Australia and New Zealand, forever, by helping people rediscover the pleasure of giving and receiving. We are working with the general public and with companies to realize this dream and, although it's a long process, it's this vision that drives us every day.

This book is an exploration to seek out exactly what it is that I am on, what drives me, what I am passionate about and what has spurred me to do the things that I have done and continue to do.

Please enjoy it.

Foreword

The rise of women entrepreneurs is the business story of our generation. It's odd that so little has been written about it. Business magazines and newspaper sections still focus relentlessly on the same old guys and the same old ideas. Even venture capitalists, who pride themselves on spotting the next big thing, have missed the next big trend.

It's not surprising that Naomi Simson should be leading the way. Like her counterparts around the world, she has recognised that the shibboleths of business are there to be questioned, not taken for granted. She brings to her company and to her writing a fresh eye, a questioning mind and a wholesome, genuine respect for customers. She knows what so many business leaders and employees forget: that customers are the only source of revenue in a business, that everything else is an expense. If you don't love your customers, you have no business being in business.

Studies around the world confirm what Naomi writes about: that women run great companies because they don't think of service as demeaning, that women are profoundly in touch with their market because, in almost all spending, they are the market. Women entrepreneurs bring to their roles as leaders an intrinsic ability to see how all the pieces fit together and how consistency between them is essential to business health. With attitudes like that, why wouldn't women do well?

In the United States, women entrepreneurs are now building companies, profits and jobs faster than business as a whole – even though they get less in the way of institutional funding. That example is, gradually, being replicated around the world. What it shows us is that in women business-owners lies a powerhouse of fresh thinking and new ideas that the business world badly needs. What's perhaps even more thrilling is that these women are also having fun, working according to their own values and principles. They are what we always suspected: work doesn't feel like work when you're doing something you love, in a way that you can respect.

For generations now, women have lapped up business books, absorbing the wisdom of male business gurus. We've been eager to learn and we have learned. But now we have a lot to teach – wisdom learned not in the library but out there in the real world, leading real business success. Men and women both have a lot to learn from Naomi Simson's success – and the business world as a whole will do better when it sits up and pays attention.

Margaret Heffernan

Margaret Heffernan is a high profile American entrepreneur, CEO, writer and keynote speaker. Her motto: "Let's not play the game, let's change it."

chapter 1
A Lifetime Of 'Nos'

So why did a marketer with more than 15 years experience suddenly throw it all in to run an experience-based gifting company, something she knew nothing about, on the internet, which she knew even less about?

I wanted to prove that marketing alone, correctly based on your people and on your customer and supplier experience, really does work. I knew that I needed to create my own environment in which to prove this, so I could guide it and have real influence from the word go and not be at the mercy of other people's management.

How did I get to the point where I needed to prove myself and where I was ready to turn my back on what I knew and head into the unknown? It was a lifetime of 'Nos' really.

If you look at a baby, you see a being of infinite possibility. What road will they take, who will they meet and what experiences will they have? Anything is possible for that child. At what point do we start limiting what we think we can do? Is it when we get a big 'NO' from a school teacher or parent?

Furthermore, where did all this negativity come from and what impact has it had on society?

It seems that people in business, and traditionally people in the public sector, are taught to say 'No' as their first response to a request. It is really hard to find someone who can say, "Yes! What a great idea, let's run with it, make a difference, take a risk, be entrepreneurial."

Throughout my life, I've been on the receiving end of many 'Nos.' Far from being deflated, I somehow twisted these 'Nos' into positives and used them to spur me on to better things. I believe that each of us has the power to choose what role, if any, our past experiences will play in our future. I've chosen to make them a big part as I know they've shaped who I am today.

So now it's my opportunity to say thank you to the many people who said 'No' to me along the way, who said, "Your ideas are just not possible – it cannot be done." I have never been someone who likes being told what to do. So if you've ever told me, "No, you cannot do that," like it or not I probably gave it a try anyway!

It is not as if my life has been surrounded by negativity, in fact quite the contrary. I have wonderfully supportive family, friends and colleagues. I am by nature extremely positive. I have always seen the glass as half full, and the good in everything and everyone. But the word 'No' has spurred me on to take on unreasonable tasks and projects. So now you know how I work – tell me I cannot have something and I will make sure the opposite happens.

Where the No began

As a child I wanted to be an artist, to paint, draw and have a professional career in the arts. At some point my art teacher said to me, "You are very talented but I can see you starving in a garret. No, you will not survive as an artist in your lifetime." However truthful, I did not like being told that I would never be a successful artist, and starving had absolutely no appeal at all! I was only a teenager but I thought there had to be some way to combine my artistic 'talents' with a career.

At that time, I loved the television program *Bewitched* with Elizabeth Montgomery. All she had to do was wiggle her nose and our witch, Samantha, could get whatever she wanted. It was not Samantha however that I related to. "When I grow up I want to be Darren," I mused. "He works in advertising, he gets to draw pictures all day and he gets paid for it." So this was my introduction to advertising and marketing. "I'll show them," I thought, those teachers who said, "No – you will not be successful." I'll go off and make a difference with my artistic talents by bringing great products to market and promoting them successfully.

Immediately after I finished my Bachelor of Commerce degree at the University of Melbourne I was fortunate to work in New York for IBM and then travel to Europe and work for another computer company in Denmark. I felt ready to change the world armed with my great marketing talents. Every young graduate thinks they know everything and I was no different.

My first job on my return to Australia was with a professional services firm. I was the Marketing Officer. This firm had just been through a merger and my job, or how it was sold to me, was to work on the 'brand development' of this newly merged firm. What this really meant was my job was to clean out the databases of the two organisations to have one clean list of contacts. This does not sound like such a big thing but in those days it took me more than nine months to do. There was no opportunity to contribute marketing ideas.

The marketing partner of the firm was so pleased when I finally completed this task that he took me to lunch to celebrate, as that's what you did in the 1980s. After the lunch I sat in his office while he delivered me my next brief; the writing of a newsletter to go to this newly-created database.

Aside from feeling deeply disappointed that I still wasn't going to be able to contribute any 'real' marketing input, I was suddenly overwhelmed by a wave of nausea. I was compelled to rush from the partner's office to the ladies' room with my hands over my mouth. I had had a bad oyster at lunch and I was violently ill. I was so embarrassed and humiliated. I was supposed to be taking a brief but I hadn't had the opportunity to ask any questions or contribute at all!

When I returned to the office the next day the partner asked, "Why didn't you tell me you were feeling ill?" I wanted to say, "Well I couldn't get a word in edgeways!" but managed to mumble a polite reply. In fact, it did not matter that I had been ill.

The point was that I never had the chance to contribute my ideas. This organisation said, "No, we do not want you to be creative and contribute your ideas, we just want you to do what we ask you to!" which is all well and good but I wanted to change the world using my creative talents and I was beginning to see that this was not going to happen in a professional services firm.

'No, we are not interested in what you want to contribute."
Lesson learned: Why have talented people if you have no intention of listening to them or nurturing their initiative?

I spoke to friends and family and also to Neil Elliott, one of the partners in the consulting side of the firm, who acted as a great sounding board and mentor. He said, "If you really want to have a career in marketing you have to go and be a Product Manager somewhere and you must work for an organisation that spends a lot of money on advertising." I agreed. Surely a company that spends money on advertising would be passionate about marketing.

I found out which companies spent money on advertising, and I pitched myself to several organisations, packaging up my CV and delivering it in a fruit basket with some catchy line about 'fresh ideas' and being eager to contribute. I sent out three to the most senior marketing executives in these publicly listed companies. I got three interviews and ultimately three offers. I chose the job not based on the salary. In fact the job I selected paid considerably less than the other two offers. I chose the company that I was really passionate about, interested in what they did and where the company had come from.

I was ecstatic to join Ansett Australia as a Product Manager (I had many roles within Ansett, ultimately becoming the Marketing Manager of Frequent Flyer and Golden Wing). When I chose Ansett, Sir Reginald Ansett was still spoken about as one of Australia's great entrepreneurs. I thought, "Now I am working for a truly marketing focused organisation that listens to its customers."

I was amazed that after a few days at Ansett, I still did not yet have a PC on my desk. I asked my manager when it would be delivered. "But why do you need a PC when we have the typing pool?" was the response. "You simply dictate what you want to have written into this machine, then the next day it comes back, you make corrections, then the day after that it comes back again." I thought, "It cannot seriously take three days just to produce a document." It did. Given that I had come from technology-focused companies this was an absolute shock to me.

"No, you cannot have the tools you need to be efficient and effective to get the job done."
Lesson learned: You have great people being unproductive if they don't have the tools they need.

One of my first assignments was to discover how many contact points a customer had with the airline. The airline was planning to roll out a new product and needed to consider all of these touch points. I discovered that there were 23 potential people that could impact the customer's experience. This was way before the days of the Internet, electronic tickets and self check-in. I was so excited to discover how the customer experienced the airline, and I presented my findings and suggested strategies for improvement to management.

Management said to me, "Do you realise you would have to speak to 11 unions to get this product enhancement through? You go and worry your pretty little head about something else." I was shattered, devastated. There were tears too. I was so passionate about making a difference to the airline and I couldn't believe that management wasn't prepared to tackle the customer experience.

But I forged on. A while later as Marketing Manager of Golden Wing (prior to Frequent Flyer being launched) I would call each of the top 10 customers, measured by kilometres flown. They were so surprised to hear from someone at the airline. "Who are you?" they would say. "I'm the Marketing Manager and I just wanted to call to say thank you for your business. It is much appreciated and we noticed." Sometimes they would tell me about what it

i want what she's having

was like to be such a frequent customer or about some aspect of the service. I would then pass that information on to the relevant area, however I had very little influence or ability to ensure that actions were taken.

Until that phone call was made, these people were just faceless beings in a reservations system, but we made them feel important and valued. And I'm positive that they told a few friends or colleagues that they had received a personal phone call from the airline; "You won't believe who called to say thanks – Ansett! I'm amazed they noticed."

Some months into the role we established the Golden Wing Board of Advisors. This was a group of customers who travelled a lot and we met once a quarter. I welcomed all the attendees at each meeting, offering them a token gift to show our appreciation for taking the time to contribute their ideas. I was also there to listen to how they viewed the customer experience. It was the small things that often resonated the loudest, such as calling people by their name when they arrived at the lounge. Everyone loved Bernie at Sydney Golden Wing Lounge because he always welcomed them by name. They felt important and noticed.

Ansett did do a lot of work around its internal culture spending money on cultural change programs and employing the services of external management consultants. Ultimately the directive on 'culture' had to come from the top, and Ansett needed a leader that was truly committed to customers. Unfortunately, during the three years that I was an employee of Ansett there was no such leader. I know that there were many people within the organisation who did love the customers but ultimately the unions had greater power than the customer experience.

> "No, we are not interested in the customer experience. We are interested in what is easier to implement."
> Lesson learned: Without happy people in an organisation it is very hard for a customer to have a happy experience with the business.

I knew that my next move had to be to a company that was truly entrepreneurial and committed to its customers. I sought out Apple Computer Australia and I was thrilled to join as a Marketing Manager, although I managed to work for Apple at the only time that its co-founder Steve Jobs didn't. On my first day I was sitting quietly at my desk and someone said, "I'm so glad you're here. We've got a warehouse full of PowerBooks. Have you any idea how to shift them?" I didn't.

The Marketing Communications Manager called in the advertising agency to assist. They had 'the perfect solution', which was to shoot an advertising campaign that took them to New York, London and Paris showing people using Macs all over the world. From memory, the production budget was about a million dollars – a far cry from the simplicity of the more recent campaign.

I often ask if anyone remembers that advertising campaign but I always get blank looks. The ad ran so infrequently, there was only a tiny media budget and the products were superseded almost immediately. The 'perfect solution' was not so perfect after all.

I learned a lot about advertising at Apple; what worked, what didn't, how to make a marketing budget look a lot bigger than it really is and what NOT to spend money on.

I also learnt to do a few things very, very well, be spectacular, take risks, be innovative and to do what others wouldn't dare to do.

Because head count was always a contentious issue at Apple, I observed that the team leaders were very adept in 'extending' their teams without increasing the head count. And I don't mean by using contractors. Apple used fantastic, small, nimble, innovative agencies to support the business; for instance, a small PR firm, research house, design studio and direct marketing agency. It also had a global advertising agency arrangement. Each of these was very focused and had specific talents.

Unlike any other organisation I had known Apple also engaged its suppliers as if they were Apple employees. Company celebrations included the marketing suppliers and they were also part of planning sessions and technology briefings. Apple knew the importance of suppliers and partnerships in its overall success.

"No, you cannot have additional people to assist you." Lesson learned: Honour your suppliers, truly engage them in your purpose, make sure that you have shared values and you will be far larger and more successful than you ever imagined without the head count.

Apple was renowned for its regular restructuring. I had many bosses and many marketing roles in my three years there. I loved the Apple culture and the product, but in the end I resigned because I was dealing with a boss I could not stand. He had been brought in from a manufacturing background, was much older than the rest of the management team, had no experience in fast-growth or innovative businesses and did not demonstrate the Apple values. There is a widely shared belief that people don't resign from companies, they resign from managers. And this is exactly what happened to me. Many of my peers left around the same time and it was the end of an era. Most went off to run their own show in some form or another. They had caught the entrepreneurial bug from Apple.

"No, you cannot stick to one project and see it to fruition. We will keep moving you around."
Lesson learned: Know what you are there to do in a day and allow time to see the results of your labour of love.

I am perpetually excited and positive about each of my new roles. Following Apple, I was wooed to a small firm and I jumped at the chance to make a really big difference to this small business. When I joined this firm they had no brand or particular identity. Given that the business was in colour publishing it needed a colourful and memorable brand identity. Its existing look was merely a blue Times Roman word. As a marketer I've found the job is so much easier if there is consistent, memorable branding on all communication.

I engaged a design studio and they came back with a fantastic icon and brand implementation plan. I presented it to my boss, the founder and owner of the business. He said, "That's interesting; let me take it home to think about it." He returned the next day and said, "My seven-year-old son

i want what she's having

NO, YOU DO NOT KNOW WHAT IS BEST. AD HOC PERSONAL OPINION IS RIGHT. LESSON LEARNED: MAKE A STAND FOR WHAT YOU TRULY BELIEVE IN AND IF IT MAKES COMMERCIAL SENSE YOU WILL WIN OUT IN THE END.

said it was 'fishy-wishy-washy'. He just doesn't like it." You cannot imagine my upset that my 10 years marketing experience was being pitched against a seven-year-old boy who was not in the target market.

I was devastated, because as a truly passionate person I get emotionally upset when something I've put my heart and soul into backfires. "It's his business, he can do what he wants with it," I had to rationalise to myself.

Why did I get so upset? After all, I was still being paid whether he wanted to listen or not. I know that it's because I have never been a half-interested person. I have always played at more than a hundred percent in anything I do. My father has been a great inspiration, saying to me throughout my childhood, "If you are going to do something, do it properly." I still hear his voice in my head regularly.

I finally had to say to my new boss, "If you want me to be a true marketer then you are going to need to listen to what I have to say. It is not about your personal taste or mine. Marketing is about what will resonate with our customers and prospects, what they will notice and remember. It's about maximising the small marketing spend that we have." I think it was the talk about money that finally got him over the line. In the end the branding was very successful. I think he even grew to like it!

After the colour publishing stint ended, I had this great idea that I would leave corporate life, become a marketing consultant, people would pay me lots of money to learn from my marketing wisdom, and as a result of paying for that advice, they would be quick to implement all these great ideas. I have often laughed that if I had not become a

i want what she's having

mother I would never have thought to start my own business. Being a mother brings a completely different set of challenges, especially teaching you to juggle priorities, and I discovered that I was actually quite good at this.

I established Bright Marketing, a marketing consultancy business, ensuring that it had a bright, colourful and memorable logo. Anyone who has been kind enough to listen to me will know that I claim to create a pretty good marketing plan. So as a freelance marketer I set about producing fabulous marketing plans for my new clients. They had at least 47 action items in them, with time scales and budgets. I included activities to create awareness, build consideration, make sure that product became preferred, advised how to close the customer loop and how to create loyalty.

One of my biggest gigs was working in the area of digital printing for Fuji Xerox, a connection which ended up coming in very handy when I started RedBalloon Days down the track. I regularly fell in love with my clients' products, whether they were colour printing machines, software applications, a typing tool or even a professional services firm. I even named a printing engine Dexter to give it more personality so customers could relate to it but it was different this time; I was on the outside looking in. I was the one that they had come to for 'the answer' and the answer was never "No" it was always "Yes, anything is possible. It just takes time and money."

Being a marketing consultant had its share of frustrations. Of all those marketing plans I produced, most clients would implement just three or four of my 47 action points. They would often say, "Well, we've done marketing now." I would argue that marketing is a journey. It is not a single activity, communication piece or promotion.

"No, I will not implement all or even half of the marketing plan. I will do the bits that look easy."
Lesson learned: It is not the size of the budget that counts. It's what you do with it that matters.

Marketing is about continually listening to your customers and discovering what they heard, learned, liked and loved. What were they delighted by? Then you fine-tune the product, service or customer experience, learn more and then fine-tune again, each time ensuring that the marketing message is authentic and related to the customers it set out to engage.

Working on the outside just was not what I expected it to be. I had no influence over direction, real strategy or allocation of resources. The 'brilliant' marketing plans I created for clients would be reduced to a few elements, maybe at best some on-going activities. I was not making the sort of difference I wanted to make to these businesses. Some just wanted to tick the box to say they did marketing. I remember one client wanted to appear in the Financial Review because that is what his friends read, not what his customers read. I began to think that marketing was all about ego, all about "I've got a bigger budget than you, so I'm more important."

I lost my passion for other people's businesses. I was simply over it and my positivity was spent. The real world just was not interested in my creativity and enthusiasm. There were other more pressing business issues for my clients.

> Lesson learned: As a marketer, no matter where I sat within or outside of an organisation, I just couldn't influence enough of the customer experience. I was not responsible for much of the stuff that really mattered.

Once I'd come to this realisation, I knew it was time for a career change. It was time to hang up my boots and do something different after more than 15 years as an internal and external marketing adviser, playing with the four Ps – Product, Price, Place and Promotion. I was over it, yet I knew that surely there was a way to fulfil my life's wish to use my creativity for the greater good.

Anyone who has worked in corporate life will have had similar experiences to mine. Corporations are not perfect beings, however it is not whether mistakes are made, or whether calamities occur; it is what is done about them. It is the values and the essence of the business that counts.

My time in corporate life, despite all these frustrations, was thrilling. It is more than a decade since I had a boss. And in all fairness I know I was a very challenging employee. I could never sit still. There was always another idea, a better way of doing things that I had imagined, some information I did not yet know and needed to discover. I'm sure my colleagues and bosses didn't always love working with me either. I would become so passionate about whatever project I was working on that I couldn't necessarily see other people's point of view, or take into account other commercial pressures of the organisation. I had my view of the world but as I now know that is just one opinion, which does not necessarily make it more relevant than someone else's. I got noticed for my hard work and for being very focused. But really, as I recently admitted to a fellow entrepreneur, I'm probably unemployable. I'm too passionate.

"No, it is not about your likes and dislikes. Your creativity was not meant to be fulfilled as a marketer."
Lesson learned: It is up to me to create my future. It is up to me to make the difference.

I wanted to become a CEO of 'something' so that I could create an organization that had a 'YES' culture, that listened to its customers, encouraged innovation from its people and used feedback to evolve and develop and enhance the product and therefore the customer experience.

Now what would that look like? How would I make it work? Oh, and what on earth would I actually sell?

i want what she's having

chapter 2
The Lift Off

Knowing that I wanted to be a CEO and doing something about it were two completely different things. I had plans and ideas, and I continued to run Bright Marketing as I pondered the universe and its infinite possibilities.

One of the ideas I came up with was having a boutique for beautiful papers and paper products, but I never did anything about it. I had an idea of running marketing educational seminars, but never did anything about that either. I had the idea of running a virtual art gallery, but this idea never got off the ground.

The idea for RedBalloon Days actually came from one of my Bright Marketing clients. He wanted to bring the UK experiences agency *Red Letter Days* to Australia and approached me for some marketing input.

When he came to me with the idea, there was no initial excitement from me, more mild enthusiasm or curiosity. I just thought, 'That could be fun, I might put a bit of my time into it.' So armed with the idea, I wrote the first marketing plan, dated 1 April 2001 – April Fools' Day. That should have been an omen, but I was too engrossed in the possibilities, I loved the concept and the idea of doing something completely new. Initially I felt that we were setting out to conduct an experiment, to test whether a company could be 'successful' simply by listening to its people and its customers and focusing on what would get people talking.

We set up a company structure, with my husband, Peter, and I as equal partners together with this client of mine and his wife. Essentially we were all working on this as a hobby while still holding down our full-time jobs. When we started it was literally the four of us and Renee Walliker, my assistant from Bright Marketing, sitting around the kitchen table in my Sydney home. We fleshed out all the resources we would need, who would do what and how it would all fit together. The two couples each kicked $25,000 in to the kitty and decided that was our slush fund from which we would have to launch the website, get the products and do some promotion.

Peter is an accountant by trade and he did all the legal contracts and set up shareholder agreements and created the company. I worked with the designers from my marketing company Bright Marketing, wrote copy and did marketing-type promotional stuff, including designing the first website. Our other business partners went off and outsourced suppliers like web developers, a printing house to print the vouchers and experiences to form the content for the website.

After about six months of working on this 'RedBalloon experiment' in our spare time, one of our business partners announced that he had been offered a management buy-out of the UK-based firm he was working for. He said it was too good to pass up, that he did not have the time to dedicate to our project and wanted out.

I had to make a decision – do I take on this project full time and really try to make it work? I'd already begun to realise that if this baby didn't get some real love and attention she wasn't going to fly. Of course this would mean that I would have to close down Bright Marketing, which at that time was making good money and paying me a regular salary, and take a big risk with this new concept with no salary, no customers, and no income; just a mountain of expenses, a big idea and lots of possibility.

i want what she's having

Up until this moment it really had only been an idea. Action would make it reality and quite frankly that was an extremely daunting idea, however a great idea is worth nothing if you're not prepared to take a risk and make it a reality. So with the second-hand Bright Marketing computers, some savings, Renee and a work experience student, I said, "Let's go for it!".

Lesson learned: You can be a victim of circumstance or you can choose your future.

In the UK, the experiences businesses were based on catalogues and call centres. This was not going to work in Australia, so we came up with another plan which fulfilled our need to serve the vastness of Australia. We took the business online and created an internet-based experiences company.

As the marketing brains of the business, I focused my energies on coming up with a name. I literally paced up and down my backyard trying to think of a name, particularly one that we could get a URL for. I remembered the wonderful Oscar-winning children's movie *The Red Balloon*. Upon further research I discovered that it was a short movie made in 1956 and that the story was so befitting to my new business venture. A red balloon befriends a little Parisian boy and after many incidents he is carried off by a bunch of balloons to experience an amazing adventure. For me, a red balloon has always been a symbol of happiness in a grey day, which I felt was the essence of this wonderful children's story. So RedBalloon became the inspiration for our new little business.

The word 'Days' was added because it implies that we provide 'days to be remembered'. Also, we originally did not have the www.redballoon.com.au URL. Technically RedBalloon is the registered company and we sell our customers 'a RedBalloon Day'. The name may not immediately describe what we do but it's a pretty hard name to forget! It is memorable and has vivid images associated with it. My vision is that in 10 years time, anyone who sees a red balloon will smile and remember a great time they had on a RedBalloon Day.

Lessons learned: The naming of a business or product is critical. You can waste a lot of money on a made-up name, or you can have a name that describes the business but is also forgettable. To capture the community's imagination and create interest in something that evokes some level of emotion or attachment makes the launch so much more straightforward. Strong visual images together with a sense of relatedness make it easy for people to recall who you are and what you do. We all love a story.

But it still takes a concerted marketing effort to create these memorable associations with the brand. I learnt this when I was presenting to about 600 people at a big event on the Gold Coast and I was having a quick chat to one of the staging people just before I was to go on stage. He said by way of farewell, "Good luck with the charity!" Clearly he

i want what she's having

had never heard of RedBalloon Days. On another occasion I had a woman come up to me at a trade show and say, "I always sleep my baby on his side" – obviously confusing us with SIDS Red Nose Day. I guess we still have to work on that brand marketing.

Contrary to popular belief, RedBalloon was not destined for success from the word go; far from it. Thanks to a series of disasters it very nearly failed in its early days. RedBalloon is, in truth, the result of a lot of people's passion, faith, dedication, innovative thinking and marketing … and a fair amount of pure bloody-mindedness!

Getting it on to the market was riddled with disasters. There were so many hurdles to get over including outside forces and circumstances out of my control, together with my own lack of knowledge.

Firstly, the initial website was a disaster. I had trusted an outsourced web development company to build the website, and it was so poorly built and so badly designed that I think it actually drove customers away! It was red with black writing which made it virtually impossible to read and it was 'framed' so you could never find the same experience again. I'm fairly sure there was no search function either. It also had one of those landing pages where the only text that appears is 'Click here to enter' which is useless if you want search engines to index the site.

Secondly, in my wonderful marketing plan there was no mention of online marketing, the internet, search engines or any other web-based activity. I knew absolutely nothing about online marketing – it sounds silly now but I remember thinking, "Oh I'm a bit old to learn all of that new-fangled Internet stuff."

Third, I was launching a dot.com company immediately after the dot.com crash where many people had lost a lot of money. The world was clearly not interested in another business launching on the Internet and I honestly thought that we were too late to the market. I was devastated when David Jones closed down their online store. I thought if DJs can't see a future in online, what hope have we got? It was not until many months later that I realised I wasn't investing in this business for now, I was investing in it for five years time when the internet would really come of age.

Fourth, we launched on October 1, 2001, three weeks after September 11. The world was in turmoil and I honestly thought that we would never sell anything. There was nothing in the media but gloom and doom for months on end and no one was in the mood for fun and exciting experiences.

Lastly, we planned to launch RedBalloon via email in late 2001 and had worked really hard on gathering a list together of people who were interested including friends and acquaintances, and planned to send them an email. Unfortunately a junk test email went out to the whole of our precious database by accident because the external developers had set up an automatic email schedule in error.

Recipients of this horrible test email thought that we had emailed them a virus. We got relegated to the junk mail folder. I'm not sure if we were actually blacklisted but we were pretty close to it.

I was beside myself. It was a massive setback. Apart from the fact that I looked like an idiot because a lot of my friends and colleagues were on that list, no customers were ringing, I had no budget and the website was not working. I was flattened. I would literally stare at the computer and

i want what she's having

think, "Now what do I do?" Two days later I sent another email saying, "We're really sorry you got something untoward. What we were really trying to tell you was this ..." But to be honest I think it took us over a year to recover from that initial bungle.

All these elements seemed to be working against us and I was in the driving seat. I had promised that it was going to be different, that I was going to create a great company and so far I was only going backwards. By asking the crucial question, "How am I responsible?", I could live free of the blame game but I was ultimately accountable for choosing the external web development supplier, and also not understanding the sensitivity of this new technology that we were developing. It was up to me to change things.

I was once sharing this disaster at a speaking engagement and I asked my regular question, "Did anybody see the website when we launched?" Usually no hands go up. This day one did, but I chose to ignore it. Afterwards I asked the guy if he really had seen the site, because we didn't really have many customers back then. I almost knew all of our visitors on a first name basis. He replied, "Yes, I was studying multimedia at the time at UTS, and my lecturer brought your website in as an example of the WORST website he had ever seen." I was glad that I hadn't asked for that response during the session!

Lessons learned: Don't be afraid to take risks. Be dead scared instead! There is not a day that goes by that I don't ask myself, "What if?". And I have never forgotten the early days when I would look on our website and say "No customers today – maybe tomorrow." I embrace the fear and ask: "What is the worst thing that could happen? Did anyone get hurt? Did we have fun? Did we make a difference?" If so, then it is all worth it. Being afraid is part of growing a business. Not being ruled by fear is what makes us entrepreneurs.

In the early days our website was just an online brochure and we didn't have any money for a proper launch. We just turned it on and went live … and the wait began.

I like to say now there is no power in hope, but I was living on hope during that time. The business was in the front room of my home in Balmain, and I was working all hours of the day and night and working harder than I ever had before. But it wasn't translating into results in the form of paying customers. I used to go and look at my computer regularly to see if anybody had visited. I would sort of gee myself up and say to myself, "If there is no one there, it doesn't mean that there will be no one there next time." And so I kept going, not necessarily surviving on false hope but you just never knew. I would often live in a fantasy world that maybe I could log on and there would be a hundred customers, or a thousand. It was disheartening but I didn't lose hope.

It was a long scary wait between the time we came up with the idea of the company in February, 2001, the launch in October, 2001 and the time of our first order on December 5, 2001.

i want what she's having

"NEVER GIVE IN - NEVER, NEVER
NEVER NEVER, IN NOTHING GREAT
OR SMALL, LARGE OR
PRETTY, NEVER GIVE IN EXCEPT
TO CONVICTIONS OF HONOUR
AND GOOD SENSE.
NEVER YIELD TO FORCE; NEVER YIELD TO THE
APPARENTLY OVERWHELMING
MIGHT OF THE ENEMY

WINSTON CHURCHILL
OCTOBER 29, 1941
TO THE BOYS AT HARROW
CHURCHILL'S OLD PUBLIC SCHOOL

I still remember it. Damien Chown bought a mind balance massage for Scott Hedge. The message on that very first RedBalloon voucher read, "Relax, unwind and have a great birthday." The total cost was $106.50 – we made $10. But that first order kicked off the process of changing gifting in Australia and New Zealand forever.

I called Damien to thank him. The order number was not actually order #1 because we'd done test orders so he didn't know he was the first, and I didn't want to tell him that. Instead, I called him to say, "Thanks for thinking of us, that is wonderful. Scott will have a wonderful time."

I could never, ever have imagined during that long two and a half months waiting for that first order that we would become such a success. I would dream, but it was in the realm of fantasy rather than being visionary.

Even after that first order it wasn't as if RedBalloon was a fully-fledged money-making business. It was 15 months before I could even consider paying myself anything. I had taken a five-fold pay cut to run RedBalloon.

What that first order did do for us was to affirm there must be more people like that, and we just had to find them.

In our first year, we approached ninemsn about getting a profile on their shopping site. We paid $5,000 which bought us a tenancy on ninemsn and with that we got three homepage inclusions per month and they put an image and description about our product on their website.

It resulted in a trickle of traffic but we did other clever things by the end of that first Christmas. We had 2,000 people on our database by then. To attract more traffic to our website we decided to run a competition, offering a massive prize containing all 50 products – so it would have

29

i want what she's having

"WE ARE NOT CREATURES OF
CIRCUMSTANCE, WE ARE
CREATORS OF CIRCUMSTANCE.

BENJAMIN DISRAELI

been worth about $50,000! Our wonderful suppliers came on board and ninemsn did the promotion. It was a great success.

We worked so hard in those early days. I remember one night I thought, "I've been working so hard but tonight I'm going to sit down and watch TV. I'm not going to work at all; I'm just going to relax!" There was a new program on that everyone was talking about and I was going to treat myself and watch it. I was on the couch for about 10 minutes when Peter came and stood in front of the TV, looked at me intently and said, "Do you realise just how much money you are losing?" That was the end of the TV show, and the beginning of some drastic changes, of us working out exactly how we could cut some costs to actually make some money. It was painful but my husband had a point.

Our first suppliers

Just because you have a great concept does not mean that anyone is even slightly, remotely interested in buying it. I'm not saying that people were giving us platitudes, it's just that we were not top of mind, and we had no lasting impression or authority.

We were developing a completely new market for gifting and doing things differently, doing things that had never been done before. There was no reason for suppliers to believe that we would deliver on our promise to drive lots of business their way.

We launched in NSW with 50 NSW-based experiences on the website. How did we even get 50 suppliers? It was

i want what she's having

tough! We looked at sites in the UK and said, "What have we got in Australia to match?" and then set about trying to find them. We used the Yellow Pages to find potential suppliers and then one of the original business partners went and tried the experiences out. Most of them said, "You want us to do what?" We would show them pictures of what the website was going to look like and the mock-ups and they were saying, "Yeah, yeah, yeah. We've seen it all before."

Initially the experiences we sought out were ones that were as close to those offered in the UK or those which were the subject of a 'craze'. Kite surfing was huge at one stage but we don't sell a lot of kite surfing now. People were using the experiences we were selling to trial them before they bought their own equipment.

Many of the suppliers were referred to us by other suppliers who were already dealing with us. Take our hot air balloonist; he is a champion hot air balloonist and he was really helpful about steering us in the right direction and saying, "These are the people you should deal with."

It was literally like pulling teeth with many of the suppliers though. It was a case of approaching 10 suppliers just to get one on board. People would say to us, "We would love to be on your website. It sounds like a great idea" and then nothing. At times we felt like screaming, "We just want to sell your stuff! Give us the contract back!"

We found the bigger the organisation, the harder they were to deal with. I was speaking to our merchant gateway supplier in the early days and he said, "You have no idea how many people come to us and say 'We've invented the next best e-commerce website on the planet after Amazon, so be nice to us and give us a great deal.' Most are not even around in 12 months."

The smaller organisations took us on and figured they had nothing to lose. They did take a risk, but eventually we got to make mammoth differences to their businesses.

The issue was that although these suppliers were brilliant (often World Champions!) at delivering their experiences, none of them had any idea about online selling, not that we did either. Most of their business came from people who could 'sense' what it was they were offering or else they were referred from the travel industry. For instance, if someone wanted to try kite surfing then they might be driving along and see someone else doing it; they'd look at the wind, get a feel for the harness and assess whether it would work for them. But selling online you cannot touch, feel or know what the experience is going to be like. So the words and images are absolutely critical.

Initially we assumed that the suppliers could articulate their experiences sufficiently and provide enough detail to put on the website. But they couldn't to the degree that we needed and neither could we. We did not know what people needed to know. How tall are you? How much do you weigh? There were all sorts of questions that we could not have anticipated. The only people who knew what they wanted to know were the customers. So given that I egotistically wanted to run a business based on the customer experience I thought I had better start to gather and listen to their feedback.

What we did was create a closed loop by creating a way of hearing directly back from the participant with a follow up 'How was it for you?' email after each experience.

The results of the survey then appeared on the intranet where the suppliers picked up their bookings. So they knew what people were saying too. We viewed and reviewed the feedback, which gave us the ability to continue the dialogue with the participant. Many replies were also published on the website so other customers could see what was written. It took about eight months to get this email feedback system working efficiently, and this system is still in place five years later.

Some of the comments are hilarious, some insightful, some out of the ordinary. I remember one woman saying that she had had a wonderful Rally Driving day, however she got very hot and dirty. She was wearing white and quite frankly she was a little disappointed at the state of her outfit at the end of the day. From this feedback we updated the website copy to include 'You may get hot and dusty'. Neither the supplier nor we would ever have thought of writing that in the description.

We also made sure that the experience descriptions that appear on the website form part of our contractual relationship with the supplier of the experience. What is written is what the participant gets.

Many of our suppliers have now worked for us for years and they are brilliant at what they do. Suppliers tell me they "love RedBalloon", as after all we make good business sense for them, bringing them incremental business they would not usually have access to. Hence they take extra special care of RedBalloon participants simply because they want us to keep sending lots more customers.

Lesson learned: Authentically get the customer engaged with what it is that you do. Simply doing what is expected is not enough. Delight them with an ability to listen and act on what they say whether it is good, bad or ugly. Without it we cannot go from good to great, let alone exceptional.

In retrospect, RedBalloon's early days were a myriad of challenges, surprises, delights, experiments and lessons learned. We were certainly on track and heading in a positive direction, but we were still conscious of being on a journey, a 'ride', with the road ahead full of twists and turns and ups and downs.

i want what she's having

chapter 3

Not An Overnight Success

When people say to me now, "I wish I had thought of that" – as if the success of RedBalloon was as easy as coming up with the idea – I want to take them back in time so that they could see how desperate and at times painful that first 15 months after we launched was.

It wasn't easy and it was far from an overnight success. It was hard and to be honest there were times when I wasn't sure that we would make it as I logged on day after day to the sight of zero sales. There were a few times that I put my head in my hands and sat there and thought, "How could this be happening to me?" I didn't cry, I'm not much of a crier generally, but I did feel the pressure. It was a feeling of desperation where I literally thought, "Where do I go from here? Is there anywhere to go?"

How did I stay so positive during those early days? Why didn't I just give up after those initial disasters? Well because I'd put $25,000 of my own money into it and a lot of time and energy. Failure just doesn't sit well with me, I had to prove to myself I could do it and I hate to admit it but my ego simply wouldn't let me fail.

The challenge was to contain costs but still grow. We were working from home on second-hand computers. We had to be frugal with any cost. I got into the habit of folding the red gift packs that we used while I was watching TV or listening to the children read. It became like knitting. For three years I folded packs most nights until we changed the design.

I took to walking to meetings with red balloons attached to my briefcase. If anyone was to ask me why, I had something to tell them, something that might excite them.

Or they just might have thought I was nuts. Either way at that stage I didn't care.

Failure isn't in my vocabulary. I am a really positive person. I don't accept that "you can't have it" or "that it is not going to happen". If someone tells me "no" I respond, "Ok, great, how can I work with that to reach some level of mutual agreement?" I've always been that way and it drives people crazy. When I'm stonewalled, I always seem to think of new possibilities in a situation.

One of the many things I learnt during my early career was that success and growth stems from finding the opportunity in what is in front of you and acting upon it. Such as how can you use the same product in a different way for a different audience? If you're after a ready-made strategy that's going to guarantee you sure-fire success, I can't give you that.

I put a lot of thought into considering the audiences that RedBalloon could reach. Who would want to buy experiences? What sort of people want to make a difference to the lives of others? I came to the conclusion that there were really two distinct groups which I labelled Corporate and Consumer. It's not just about mums and dads and brothers and sisters buying as I had initially thought. I realised there was far more to be gained from targeting the corporate sector.

Many large corporations set aside budgets for rewarding and recognising their staff, but this concept was not particularly widespread at the time. Or if it was, it was a retail store voucher, a hamper or a company pen. A uniform gift for everyone, no personalisation. "How does that show an employee they are really valued?" I thought to myself.

i want what she's having

I thought if I could just get into that sector, to one big company and convince them to give experiences as rewards, to give people choice and to give them memories they will talk about, we would get some traction.

But what does it take to say "I could do that" and then do it?

We were lucky early on, to get a corporate order from Fuji Xerox primarily due to my already close relationship with them. It was our first taste of corporate sales and it felt great. But they wanted a National program and we only offered NSW-based experience. "No problem. We will be ready with national product in three months." I put my word to it, so then it just had to happen.

We went back to our supplier base and asked for referrals. Most helicopter pilots know of other helicopter pilots in other states, and many are members of professional bodies where others can be found. We basically tapped into our supplier network to find new suppliers and after much pleading and hard work an ever-growing national range was created.

The promotion ran not just for the quarter, but for six consecutive periods and it was our first real taste of corporate sales. The program started as originally planned nine months after we originally launched.

But I just needed more where that came from. I hired a part-time corporate sales person but I don't think they brought on one client, so sadly I had to let them go! This was a really hard decision but the costs were too high. It can't be that hard to sell such a great concept I thought; I needed a break, something big that would really launch us into the corporate space.

There are so many people who totally support me and therefore I have to live up to who they see me as. I made a statement that entering the corporate market was what I was committed to and so I had to act, live and breathe like I was already there.

My husband Peter has always been a fantastic challenger and supporter. He challenges me to greatness. For him "good enough never is", which means I push on. Peter has always encouraged me and has been a great mentor, although I don't always like what he says.

> "Many people have gone further than they imagined they could, because somebody else thought they could."
> Anon

He thinks that I am a good enough marketer but totally irresponsible financially. Peter, too, has had a corporate career (in fact he is ex-Coopers and Lybrand so he is quite handy with a balance sheet and cash flow forecast). He has also created and sold several other businesses. At some point after he sold one and I was up to my neck in contracts and compliance at RedBalloon, I asked him to assist (he had always been an equal share holder). Could he review this, check that, what about trademarks? I was endlessly questioning him.

I must admit having a husband with a strong accounting/finance background is invaluable. After a period of 12 months or so, there were too many questions and it became obvious that the business needed a lot more of him.

41 | i want what she's having

That was when the fun really started. The debates seemed to be daily struggles – exhausting yet insightful. It was always a battle between keeping overheads low and investing in marketing. After all, I needed to tell people we existed, how else are they supposed to find us? For instance I wanted to spend $15,000 on a trade show called the Corporate Gift Show. I thought to myself, "If I am going to have any chance to really pitch RedBalloon to the corporate market, I need to be there. No, I absolutely have to be there."

Peter pointed out that at current earnings that amount equated to 15 months revenue (not profit) and wasn't I being slightly foolish to spend that amount of money? We had a very 'heated discussion' over that one. He finally said to me "Well it's your money, Honey." "Me, foolish?" I thought. Is someone who takes risks foolish? Sometimes you have just got to jump in and swim and so I decided this event was going to be the making of RedBalloon in the corporate space.

Far from settling on a stand where we could hand out a few brochures, we called up our suppliers and had a rally car, a hot air balloon basket and a number of other real life props to adorn the stand. We were big, bold and outrageous. It was a gamble – but we looked big, we were acting as if we were big. We were living into the future that we dreamed of.

I followed up every detail, every lead, and every idea of an opportunity. Ultimately we won $500,000 worth of business over the next 12 months from the event, and we still get regular business from those that we first met at that trade show.

> "Opportunity is missed by most people because it is dressed in overalls and looks like work." Thomas Edison

Peter and I still never take any marketing spend, or other spend, within the business for granted. We push each other to the next level. I never knew our relationship could be so profound and fabulous. During the first 10 years of our marriage, I never ever, ever, ever, thought that we could work together, let alone be a powerful partnership. Now we have been working together for five years and I never stop being challenged. In fact I seek it out and I have surrounded myself with other mentors – four in fact – mostly other business people. Their insights are refreshing and it keeps me grounded.

Lesson learned: Have great mentors – learn from their experience and stick to the business principles. Mentors and coaches come in all shapes and sizes – it is a matter of listening for contribution. They tend to show up when you really need them. Give up your pride and ask for help, it won't hurt.

The trade show was a pivotal moment for us. We received orders bigger than I could have ever imagined when I first wrote the business plan. But large orders, as I was soon to discover, actually presented a whole new set of challenges, which again would force the business to grow.

From the beginning I never thought of us as a small business. We were a big business in a small agile body. We had a big plan and now we were dealing with other big companies.

Unfortunately the vision did come unstuck a few times along the way, particularly when dealing with the organisations who supplied us with services. To telcos, hosting companies and the like, we were small and therefore denied many of the privileges that big companies enjoy.

Have you ever waited on hold continuously for an hour, for someone, anyone, to answer your question, only to be re-directed three times until you can finally tell someone your website is down? You'll understand the pain we felt in the early years.

How can you tell one business from another anyway? It is not just by the size of the account surely? We are fast growing, we have different special needs but each time we get labelled a small business it actually stunts our growth.

As time went on, just because I had a few successes breaking in to the corporate market, it by no means meant the job was done. I was starting to see the infinite potential of this business; there was no way I could continue unless I invested more. Dealing with customers, suppliers, corporates, distribution channels and affiliates was becoming exhausting; it was all so exciting but it was more than I could give.

I was also getting more advice than I could handle. When we launched, Peter's brother, Stuart Simson, said, "Great idea but shame about the website." But I refused to listen because I was very protective of 'my baby' and upset at the criticism. However, as time went on I could see he had a point.

I remember one day looking at our stats and realising that we had more people in the shop at that moment than Myer probably did, but they just weren't buying at anywhere near the same rate. I recognised that my focus needed to become how to convert those visits to sales. I had no idea about functionality or usability. I could use the site easily myself because I had developed it.

Luckily ninemsn gave us some pointers in this department. They said very politely and elegantly, "You know, maybe if you just get rid of that first page that says 'skip intro', that could be an advantage. And do you know you need to have deep linking?" They were very generous with what they told us, and redesigning the website making their suggested changes really helped us. It made it easier to attract customers and to keep them. Development has now become a perpetual journey for us; I now know it is never going to be finished.

As I entered this new chapter of sophistication with the website, it was also becoming very clear I needed to hire some people.

i want what she's having

chapter 4
Discovering Our Purpose

Even though we were making headway in the corporate market and we were making some real sales through the website, there were some very basic questions that we didn't ask ourselves in the early days – maybe because we had no idea how to answer them. Firstly what did a customer look like? We did not know the difference in our audiences. There are purchasers and participants, plus suppliers, affiliates and distributors each of whom have different needs from us. Secondly what service are we providing? At the time, we thought we did everything; we sold experiences to everyone, marketed to you to buy for yourself, to you to buy for others, for groups, as holidays, wedding proposals – the list goes on. We had one foot in the travel camp, another foot in the events camp, another in recreation, in gifting and in corporate incentives.

It took almost two years to get our story straight, to find our purpose and position ourselves. And when we finally got it, it moved our realm of thinking, enabled us to create words to speak directly to our different audiences and create plans for off-shoots of RedBalloon, positioned to service these audiences in the way they wanted to hear from us.

One of the first off-shoots was the RedBalloon Corporate website. People buying birthday gifts had very different needs to someone who wanted to find out how a reward and recognition program could benefit their business. The corporate website allowed us to provide clients with lengthy information that we simply didn't have space for on the main RedBalloon site and that was irrelevant to their needs.

Next we established that one-fifth of our customers actually used RedBalloon to buy for themselves and these customers didn't want a gift voucher, they just wanted to book an experience and go and do it. We realised that a third of all calls we received were from customers wanting to book on a specific date. A gift voucher system didn't work, because they had to buy and then redeem the voucher and by the time they had done that, the availability could be gone. So another new off-shoot idea emerged, GoDo, which offers instant online booking for activities. You find an experience, choose an available date and receive instant confirmation.

But where did that leave RedBalloon? Well, it allowed us to establish what we were really about – gifting. And that's the space we now operate in – "amazing gifts for amazing people".

When we decided to stop being all things to all people life got so much easier. But then the big decision had to be made. Within the gift market, what exactly do we stand for and what is our purpose?

A certain amount of introspective assessment (soul searching) goes on before any action is taken. One must ask the simple questions first: "Why are we special? What is remarkable about what we do? What will make us different? How do our customers experience us?" The answer is not the product we sell. Sure we have an amazing range of experiences, that makes us different, but there were other people in the Australian (and New Zealand) markets who had been agents for experiences before we came along. So while the product was groovy, it was not going to set us apart. Clearly in the initial years it wasn't our badly designed website that made us special either. In fact over the course of the development of the first four versions of the website we only achieved marginal improvements each time (Version five was a complete rewrite). It clearly

i want what she's having

was not our great advertising either – we had no budget for that.

Answering the simple questions took us on a journey of discovery and the answers were not immediately identifiable. They evolved over the first two years of RedBalloon being in business. (It took me 15 months in total to realise that RedBalloon was even going to be viable). It became an exploration with the other team members, each of them feeding in their thoughts from the different customer groups they represented, and it took asking a lot of customers informally about what value we added to them.

When my purpose revealed itself I knew exactly why I got out of bed every day. I bounded in to work, excited as a kid in a candy shop: "What will we create today?", "Who do we get to talk with?", "How will we delight people?" You already know that I'm a positive person; can you then imagine what it's like when you also have answered the biggest question of all – why am I doing this?

Why do you do what you do?

It is not 'what' you do that makes the difference; it is 'why' that puts a spring in your step, a smile on your face, and gives you a sense of fulfilment. And it is the 'how' that makes a difference to others.

How did I discover our purpose? I kept asking myself the question, "So what?". We deliver great experiences – so what? We have a fantastic team – so what? We deliver lots of business to lots of suppliers – so what? These are all great things, but they are what fulfil our purpose and not the purpose itself.

I got my personal purpose first, quite simply 'I want to give people a good time, whether they work with me, for me, buy from us or are the lucky recipient of an experience.' Who said you cannot have fun in business? With so much gloom and doom in the media, I was energised by the thought of bringing some positivity to the world through what we deliver.

"Creative ideas flourish best in a shop which preserves some spirit of fun. Nobody is in business for fun, but that does not mean there cannot be fun in business."
Leo Burnett, Advertising Executive, 1891–1971

And at RedBalloon our purpose is simple, "Pleasure – our actions create amazing days to fulfil people's dreams, delight others and inspire greatness." It's actually a little more formal but it says the same thing. Because of this, the question I ask when interviewing people to join RedBalloon most often is 'Why do you want to work here?' I want to find out whether they are someone who looks at what they can give versus what they can get. I know that the team I have is very passionate about giving people a good time.

Once we had the purpose nailed, making decisions became so much easier, but the challenge was how to communicate what we were committed to, to our potential customers.

In the early days, people had never heard of us, they had no idea what we did, and we somehow expected to sell something. Imagine coming to a website and seeing something you like, you have just stumbled across it, no one

i want what she's having

referred you, it was just a text link in a Google search. What is it that will make you feel comfortable enough to pass over your hard earned cash on what looks like a good idea? It takes a leap of faith. It takes trust and as Chief Experience Officer that is what I am responsible for. Making sure not only that we fulfil on our promise by delivering an amazing experience, but more that we will delight people so that they will tell someone, not just anyone, but everyone.

Getting people to put their faith in a web interface was an incredible feat. People buying for themselves are more likely to try new things and take risks, but when they are buying for someone else, the odds of 'getting it wrong' increase and they want reassurance. I learned a very important lesson here. I thought because we were a web business, people would just transact online with us. We have an FAQ section, so why would they need to talk to anyone? Our phone number historically was very hard to find, buried in a sub-page of a page; we had no customer service team, no call centre. We couldn't possibly answer the phone. But it would ring, and it would keep ringing and although the FAQs page did tell them the answer, they just wanted to speak to someone. They wanted reassurance and to know they could trust us.

So now I have a full time team who talk to our customers all day (they are called the Pleasure Relations team!), we put the phone number on the site and we welcome customers to call. This is the only way we know our purpose is being fulfiled, from the stories we hear. More importantly, talking to our customers, letting them hear our personalities at the other end of the line, is the most effective way we can get our customers to experience us as a brand.

Having a purpose has made all the difference to what I do in a day. I'm committed to fundamentally changing gifting forever in Australia and New Zealand and I'll know if I get there because I have given myself the audacious goal of 10 per cent of the Australian and New Zealand populations having had a RedBalloon Day by 2015.

The thing is I have no idea exactly how I'm going to achieve this. But I do know that when I said that I was selling 10,000 experiences a year and only three years later it was more like 80,000. What it means is I never stop looking for innovative ways to market, promote, or distribute. I've given myself 10 years and I only have eight to go. The race is on!

'Let us not wallow in the valley of despair, I say to you today, my friends. And so even though we face the difficulties of today and tomorrow, I still have a dream ..."
Martin Luther King, Jr: "I Have a Dream". Delivered 28 August 1963, at the Lincoln Memorial, Washington DC.

Having a dream gives you something to grow into and that shapes how you live day to day. I know in order to achieve this audacious goal I have to do something every day that enables me to achieve it.

I have also worked out that I need no special visionary or magical skills to get me there, all I do everyday is make sure I 'listen' and that is what will get me there.

It's not always easy to do when your inbox is full, you are being asked endless questions and there are invoices to sign off, but I make time every week to simply listen to our customers directly. I will pick up the phone and speak to people who are calling our pleasure relations team.

Whatever they are calling about, whether it's good or bad, I find it fascinating. With every phone call I learn something that could enhance the business.

I have never feared customer feedback! In fact I welcome it and encourage it. Everyone has gold inside. It is the ability to really listen for it that makes the difference. Some people try to hide their gold, others give it away freely.

I remember once a woman called RedBalloon wanting to speak to the 'complaints' department. I said "Oh we've never had a complaint before, but we have had lots of people providing us with a valuable contribution so that we can get even better at what we do". It shifted the tone of the conversation immediately. We listen for contributions, not problems: how can we quantify, then improve, enhance and develop based on what we have learned? I think it is this ongoing cycle that not only keeps us on our toes but presents us with some of the best business opportunities.

Because we know that the customers are where the gold is, we don't wait to hear from them. We have always been proactive and that still continues today. After each experience we send every participant a "How was it for you?" email survey and they get read every day, looking for comments, for improvements, for anything we can use to make the lives of customers easier.

Listening is all it takes to create a customer-centric business; it's just finding the time to do it that takes the work.

This is just one of the many valuable things we learned in the early formative years. With a clear direction now guiding the way, we were free to focus on the core strength of our business – our people – and to home in on the values that really make RedBalloon unique.

i want what she's having

chapter 5
Valuable Values

We call ourselves 'RedBallooners' but what does that mean? We say that we are different, special, not like other businesses, a sea change for our team members who have left large corporations. But what makes it so? It comes back to who we are as an organisation and the values that we live by. It was from the feedback and stories that we shared about the people who worked at RedBalloon that ultimately began to give substance to the notion of our values.

For instance, if I ever ask Jemma, our Marketing Manager, to do something and she agrees, she sometimes has no idea exactly how she is going to make it happen but I can be confident that she will get it done. She can always be counted on, and if something happens to get in her road then she will let me know. This realisation prompted me to ask "Do other people at RedBalloon represent the same level of integrity? Can they be counted on to do what they say they are going to do?" The answer was yes. If one of the team asks for my support they know they will never have to ask twice.

We determined that our first value was simply: **"We will do what we say we are going to do"**.

This is pervasive through every aspect of the business. The words and images on the website which describe our experiences are also driven by our values, ensuring that our suppliers also fulfil on this value of integrity and do what they say they will do.

"Hi guys, I just wanted to thank you and let you know that I have just received the Rocky Road tasting experience. The order was delivered exactly when it was due. The lady gave me a courtesy call to let me know when the item would arrive and to confirm the address. I am so extremely impressed with the service and the amazing presentation of the basket that I had to email you and let you know. Keep up the good work and thank you." Michaela Ross

During my corporate life, I remember asking many bosses to support me or assist with a particular project, only to find myself in a waiting game, wondering if and when they were going to do what they had promised. I thought about the level of trust I could create as a leader if everyone knew that if they made a request of me, they could count on me to deliver (or at least keep them informed if things don't go according to plan). What level of trust would there be in an organisation where you knew that you could count on anyone?

One of the things that I often marvel at is how generous people at RedBalloon are. Not just with customers and suppliers, but also with each other. When a new employee arrives, they are so welcoming and supportive. They are there for others, generous with their time, listen and provide information. We may well be a gift giving business so you would think that generosity is a given at RedBalloon. But you can never take any of the values for granted. This is why we listen so carefully to the stories such as the one below, and have made "**Be Generous**" our second value.

Dear Naomi,

I would like to say a very big thank you to a fellow employee of RedBalloon, Catherine. Her service was absolutely outstanding and as a result I felt confident to make a purchase with RedBalloon. Catherine was extremely patient, very friendly and understanding. Her helpfulness was more than I expected and I appreciated that very much. I think that she is a great asset to the company and a crucial contributor to the company's success. Because of her great attitude and service, I will continue to use the services that RedBalloon provide as I know and feel confident that I will be looked after. Overall, I would like to say a big thank you to Catherine and RedBalloon for their great service and hope Catherine is acknowledged for her outstanding service.

Sincerely

Liz

Having worked in organisations where the only thing that people were allowed to say was NO, we really want RedBalloon to be a YES organisation. I had seen companies where the manager or CEO becomes a total bottleneck for all decisions or where you needed to get approval to do something remarkable for a customer. This is why no matter which job function someone performs at RedBalloon, we want people to *think outside the box, to innovate and be a leader with a sense of responsibility, ownership, accountability and entrepreneurial spirit*. This is our third value and it helps to free each of us up to amaze and delight our customers, suppliers and colleagues daily.

I encourage my team to give me feedback, particularly if there has been a demonstration of 'leadership' that I am unaware of:

Hi Naomi

To give credit where credit is due, and in case you weren't aware ... it was newbie Robert who suggested we integrate Google Maps. He is an avid follower of all things Google and was the first to spot the opportunity and then got others on board the idea.

Obviously he didn't single-handedly make it happen but he was the instigator and being such an exciting and high-profile development others were keen to get involved.

Regards

Duncan

It is really important not to take ourselves too seriously. We are in the business of giving people a good time. If we are not having a good time ourselves, then we lack credibility. I've found that if you get really attached to a certain outcome, a lot of frustrated worrying docs not result in a better outcome. I learned a long time ago not to worry about what you can't impact and not to worry about the unknown.

A number of years ago Ike Bain, right-hand man to Dick Smith and author of 'The Dick Smith Way', said in a presentation "It's OK to have fun in business". I absolutely

| i want what she's having

agree, and so not surprisingly our fourth value is **"Have Fun"**. This does not necessarily mean that it's party time all the time, but we do love to celebrate, laugh at ourselves and share a joke.

Our final value stems from our commitment not to become bogged down in bureaucracy as we continue growing. Keeping the culture of innovation, flexibility, courage and 'let's give it a try' to us is summed up simply with **"Be a little dog with a BIG dog personality!"**

In the early days we would enhance our size thinking that large organisations only wanted to deal with big businesses, which is not always the case. Large organisations often like dealing with nimble, focused, organisations. Being a specialist in a niche market is attractive to any sized business. Professionalism is key, as demonstrated by the email below, from another of my team members:

Hi Naomi,

Despite the fierce resistance, Stephanie persevered and redesigned the logo which is a huge step forward in helping RedBalloon on its journey to come of age.

She has continued to impress and with her design skills and dedication taking on evolving the logo, doing brand guidelines makes us look like a big player that is being a little dog with a big dog attitude.

Thanks

Mark

"WHAT LIES BEFORE US,
WHAT LIES BEHIND US,
IS NOTHING COMPARED
TO WHAT LIES WITHIN US."
RALPH WALDO EMERSON

There are literally hundreds of examples of the RedBalloon team living the values. It is what we listen for in our recruiting program. I figure that you can teach people the technical aspects of a role, but you cannot teach them to love their fellow human beings. They either have our values or they don't.

The five values I've detailed are what make us RedBallooners. They also help us make swift decisions. Often if I'm not quite sure of the right decision to make, I ask myself 'Am I being generous?'. The answer is then simple, as the values provide a great benchmark and give us the rules for the game. Because for us it is not winning at all costs, it is how we play that makes the difference in the long term.

Values are everything to the brand

The RedBalloon team living the values is the thing that our competitors cannot copy. We know that the majority of people don't buy our product based on a price decision (if you want a cheap gift you go to Priceline). We also know that according to the Gallup Organisation only 13 percent of consumers buy products or services based on price. What people want is value, and this is where the first of our values, integrity, comes in.

Do they purchase simply because of our fabulous product range? In part yes, but I would also argue that it is the leadership we show in finding the experiences and putting them together that makes people choose us.

Is it the quality of the service we offer? Well, one has got to ask exactly how much service can be delivered if you are transacting over a website, but we work hard to ensure our personality is transparent through our website, our emails and other means of communication. People can clearly see that we are a business having fun.

Is it our speed? Customers can now order online in seconds, have the voucher emailed to them and print the voucher at home (there are other options too, but this is certainly the fastest). If there are any issues, our Pleasure Relations team is on hand to take our customers' calls. Our speed is certainly attractive to many time-poor customers, who I'm sure love the fact that they can order at any time of the day or night from the comfort of their desk or lounge room!

Overall, I believe that it is 'the experience of the experience' that makes the difference. It's the whole and complete experience our customers, clients and suppliers have when dealing with RedBalloon, and that experience is created by our people. It was a team member who said 'Let's call ourselves something different. We don't do call centre here. We create pleasure for people, hence we should be called the 'Pleasure Relations' team. You get a far different reaction from people; we know the business we are in.

Values are what make you who you are, both as an individual and as a business. After all, a business is just a whole group of people pulling in the one direction. United by a common purpose and core values which are intrinsic to all, this group still needs a leader to ensure that everything remains on track. I believe that good leadership is a key element in a successful business.

chapter 6
Being A Leader

In 2005 we were a finalist in the Telstra Business Awards. I attended a briefing session for the finalists and one of the questions that had been asked in the application was "What are the three most critical elements to your success?" The responses differed depending on the size of the business – "a great team" and "people growth and development" were more important for larger organisations for example. But one element that was missing from all of the entries was leadership. Given that the business owners fill in their own forms, I found this quite surprising.

The business owners did not write leadership in their applications because that is what they do every day, it's a given. Without leadership these businesses would not flourish.

Leadership is not management – they are two very different things. Just because you manage a team of people does not mean that you are a leader. Leadership is not determined by the role that someone plays in an organisation and does not just come from the top; it is a shared value for the entire team, with everyone given the capacity to be 'a leader' every day in their job. It's about each individual's contribution to that organisation.

This can be confusing for some people. Some people like to be told what to do and how to do something. But most people like to know they used their ingenuity and that they are able to get on with the job without waiting for a decision from someone else before they can progress with their work. If a business is well run, people should know what they are there to do in a day and be able to get on and do it. This should filter from entry-level positions throughout the entire organisation. Regardless of where employees sit in the business, they need to be able to determine the outcome of their work. This is good leadership.

I often wonder why there are not more courses at tertiary institutions on leadership. What about a Masters in Leadership, rather than a Masters of Administration? Of course we need people to manage, administer and document, but add leadership to that mix and imagine what difference it could make. Everyone at RedBalloon is encouraged to be a leader and I know that it's a cornerstone of our success.

Fear cannot stop us from our obligations as a leader. No matter how bad it gets, if we take the job it is up to us to lead. Good, bad or ugly we are responsible. As Tim Pethick, founder of Nudie Juice, said 'We are like the punching bag clowns; we just need to keep bobbing back up'. That's what leaders do. Just keep taking it and hearing contributions, then moving forward.

It's a pity that Ansett did not heed this advice many years ago when it spent many millions undertaking a 'cultural change' program called 'Reach Out', flying every Ansett employee in to one city for big motivational seminars. They thought this was a surefire way to improve employee engagement with the airline. But do you think that the General Manager when passing through an airport would stop and ask his people "How's business in your world?" or "What is the biggest frustration you have at work?" Highly unlikely. The airline was a highly unionised work force at that time and the General Managers were probably too scared to ask questions, or even speak with

i want what she's having

people, in case they faced a situation that they had no idea how to handle, or heard something they didn't want to hear, let alone say thank you personally to their staff.

Leaders don't necessarily relish the ugly stuff, the things they don't want to face up to or hear. On the inside, we might be yelling "get me out of here" but we chose to be the leader and as such we're responsible, no matter which way it goes.

"The Chinese use two brush strokes to write the word 'crisis.' One brush stroke stands for danger; the other for opportunity. In a crisis, be aware of the danger – but recognise the opportunity," John F. Kennedy Speech in Indianapolis, April 12, 1959

Leadership means different things to different people. I've invented my own four 'P's of leadership.

- People
- Purpose
- Passion
- Persistence

This is not an exhaustive list, but it provides a guide for me:

People:

Don't you hate it when someone says to you after a demi-disaster "Oh I thought that it might not work but I didn't

want to say anything because you seemed so determined."
"Ugh! I really would have listened to your ideas," you say.

"You say that now but would you really have listened?"

Michael Feiner reminded me of that children's story 'The Emperor's New Clothes'. The emperor ends up parading naked in the street because everyone buys into the story that the cloth he is wearing is so fine that you can't see it. No one says anything until a small child who does not know the story asks the simple question "Why is the emperor naked?"

There is insight for all of us in this story, whether emperor or child. I do not know all the right actions to take within my organisation. I have a fantastic group of people who all have different ideas, who have had different dealings with our customers and who have had different exposure to other successful organisations. Each of them has an opinion, and none of them is necessarily more correct than another's. My first lesson in leadership was learning to validate other people's opinions.

I want to run a business where people get listened to, particularly since that's why I left corporate life. I want to be in an environment where people feel encouraged to share ideas and where innovations are explored. I have worked in large organisations with an 'open door policy' but in reality no one took advantage of the open door as they were either too scared or didn't think it was worth the effort because nothing would come of their contribution anyway.

It is a two-way street, creating an environment of listening and responsiveness and truly honouring those who contribute. At RedBalloon we have monthly efficiency and innovation awards. Not every idea gets fulfiled but the person who nominated the idea stays informed about where

i want what she's having

the idea is up to. They might even end up the driver of that idea if it ends up being implemented.

Having said that each person in a business can be given the opportunity to be 'a leader' in their daily work, ultimately one person must be accountable for 'leading' the strategy and direction of a business. Management by committee is not leadership. And it is up to the business leader to get support for the idea, and to get others to buy into the story and to make it their own.

Purpose:

It is very easy to get out of bed in the morning if you know why you have been put on the planet. Purpose is not just for the CEO or Managing Director, it is for every person in the organisation.

A friend of mine runs a small business office support company. He said he was having difficulty getting his employees to really engage with his client's customers. Answering other businesses' phones just was not inspirational for them.

I asked the question "What business are you really in?" He said "Providing office support for small businesses." I answered "So the future of Australia is in your hands. Small business is at the heart of Australia's success and you are accountable for the first impressions of these businesses. Isn't it your job to make sure that you nurture these businesses until they grow too big for you? Then you will know that you've done a good job."

He looked at me oddly; "I've never looked at it that way." He went back to his phone team and shared the purpose, "We are responsible for the viability of small business. We are the backbone of Australia. And phone call by phone call we make a difference to the whole country. It is up to each of you." He then got them to turn it into a game with a scorecard for Australian small business success.

He said when they got their purpose the difference was phenomenal, not only to what they delivered to their clients but how they enjoyed what they did every day.

He who can thinks he can, and he who can't thinks he can't. This is an inexorable, indisputable law." Henry Ford (1863–1947)

Passion:

I recently admitted to a friend, "My problem is that I fall in love regularly," whether it be a movie I have seen, an outfit, a restaurant, a business book or a website I've found. Then of course I have to tell everyone I meet about it, and even those I have not met via my blog.

It is really hard to get people aligned on a course of action without passion. And there is no faking it. You either believe or you don't.

Think of the great leaders you know. What is it that links them all? It is not their politics or their personality. It comes back to their set of beliefs and getting others to share that belief. What links them is their ability to make a passionate stand for something and to stick to it.

There is no hiding in true leadership; no secrets, second agendas or falsities. If these things are present then you

73

have politics, not leadership. True leadership is about being straight with people, being truly authentic, real and vulnerable.

The great entrepreneurs that I have met are all driven by an unstoppable passion. And it is rarely about the money. Sometimes it is to prove something to someone. Many have gone into business with a notion of wanting to achieve financial success but for all of them, they are fundamentally driven by the difference that they, their product, service or business makes to others that really drives them. It is their passion to solve a problem profitably.

> "Success is the ability to go from failure to failure without losing your enthusiasm."
> Winston Churchill

Persistence:

Someone I know who runs another website asked me "When did you know that you would be successful?" I responded "It depends on how you define success." He said "Well, when did you turn a profit?" It took us 15 months to know that we had a market who were interested in purchasing our products and that there was a future for what we were setting out to do. He looked rather dejected at my answer. Being already three years into his project, he was beginning to ponder the question of 'if' rather than 'when'.

Fifteen months in the scheme of things is not a very long time. But when does persistence spell disaster? Is there a

"THERE IS PERSISTENCE
AND THEN THERE IS PIG HEADEDNESS,
KNOWING THE DIFFERENCE
IS THE CHALLENGE."

WINSTON CHURCHILL

formula that dictates when we should give up on our business dream? Unfortunately I can't offer any clear cut answers here but I can share with you that if we had given up on RedBalloon when it had no customers, a lousy website, an email disaster and limited suppliers then it would not have gone on to achieve our dream of changing gifting in Australia and New Zealand forever. We persevered with our idea, backed by strong persistence and passion.

People first: the leader's responsibility

I had the privilege of learning from Gail Kelly, the CEO of St George about her thoughts on leadership. It was quite clear that she genuinely cares about people. She sees her role as custodian of the St George culture and realises that people are the most important aspect of her job. She also shared her belief that the greatest gift we have is the power of choice. We are responsible.

The word Responsibility has two parts:
Response – We get to choose our response to any circumstance.
Ability – We have the ability to respond in anyway we choose.

I am the Chief Experience Officer of RedBalloon, not because we sell experiences, but because I am passionate about how anyone and everyone experiences our organisation, including staff, customers and others.

My responsibilities are two-fold in the organisation. One role is leadership and the other is building strategic external relationships. Leadership encompasses all things HR and people-related, from recruitment to planning as well as vision, and keeping everyone focused on the plan. Being the external face for the organisation is equally important as our strategic partnerships are not just big relationships; they're relationships that move RedBalloon towards its overall Big Hairy Audacious Goal (BHAG).

I have an absolutely wonderful team at RedBalloon. We grew from zero to forty people in just five years, creating a community of people who are so connected to each other and know that they can count on each other and their team leaders, and we've had fun along the way. In the early days of the company we needed 'jacks of all trades'. Renee Walliker, CEO of GoDo, often laughs that she joined as a marketer but actually got to be an accounts clerk, sales person, web producer, procurement officer, online marketer and many other things! As we grew we needed people with specialist skills and talents. When we first brought the development of our website in-house, my next-door neighbour came and did the work, and stayed for more than two years. When Kirsten Munachen, arrived at RedBalloon in 2003 for her sea-change from corporate life (referred by a friend of mine), she soon attracted others from her home state of Western Australia. There was a time when seven of the 10 people at RedBalloon were from the West.

Jim Collins in *Good to Great*, maintains that you've got to have the right people first before you can even make sure that they are in the right roles: "People first and strategy second".

When one of the team refers a potential new employee they know our company values, they know if they will fit and get along with people. This happens often, which I take as a fairly good indication that my RedBallooners like working here! We also like to develop people within our company and given the customer is the centre of our world the best place to start is in our Pleasure Relations team before moving into another part of the company later on. I'm not saying we have all the answers here. I've made recruitment mistakes, put people in roles that did not suit their strengths and we've had people resign, however I feel this is relatively few compared with other businesses. Our team spirit is very strong, even if things don't go perfectly, and we bounce back quickly. I don't give up and I will always stay committed to the individuals who make up the team.

Someone in an organisation has to make the tough calls on strategy, people and resource allocation. And sometimes you are not popular for doing so. I've found myself in this situation at RedBalloon. We had a person full of delight and excitement working in our Pleasure Relations team who was a wonderful personality and the life of any party. However her strengths just did not mesh with the obligations of the role which was very detail-oriented. After many conversations about her behaviour I had to let her go.

It was such a tough decision, particularly considering she was very close friends with many of the team, but they knew that she was not fulfilling our values. It was initially very painful, but in the long run it was best for both of us. She has gone on to get the most perfect job for her as the warm-up person for audiences at a television studio, which suits her 'big' personality well.

Occasionally there is not quite a good fit between an employee and an organisation and it's up to the leader to make the hard decision to let them go.

Doing what's in the best interests of the company is something that the leader has to stay focused on. I'm not talking about being ruthless and unfeeling towards your people or external parties you're dealing with. But you will never be able to please everyone, and it's often the leader's tough job to make decisions which are unpopular, but are for the good of the company.

Thankfully it's not all tough decisions! Being the leader of RedBalloon means that I have been able to orchestrate some significant changes in how the company operates day to day, and it's been exciting to see the positive effect of these developments, not only operationally but also emotionally on our team.

chapter 7

It's Just A Game – How Rhythm Sets You Free

In RedBalloon's early days, with a small team all in the same room, we had daily debates and no real need for meetings because all we had to do was shout across the room for an immediate response. But now with a staff of 40 people it's not the same. We've had to grow up, we've had to embrace structure and structure isn't a word that most entrepreneurs really warm to. It has connotations of being less agile, of being tied down, beholden to others and of course it sounds like a lot of meetings.

We suffered a few growing pains as we tried to get the right balance of people, meetings and who was responsible for making sure what we discussed at meetings actually happened.

Thoughts without actions are useless

As we got bigger and started to take ourselves more seriously, everything started to slow down. We became less agile, we made decisions more slowly and things took longer to develop. We realised we had too many cooks in the decision making kitchen and that we were losing sight of the fact that business is just a game. We were concerning ourselves with process and forgetting the bigger picture.

I realised we were going to need some sort of structure for decision making, a proper planning process and a way to still keep everyone in the loop. RedBallooners hate being left out and they all have to know what's going on.

To play the game we need the rules, we need a plan. You can never get to a BHAG (as coined by Jim Collins in

Built to Last) if you don't work out the steps to take to get there.

So I decided on the structure for a management team, with the team leaders being individuals who worked within different parts of the business and who I believed were best equipped to lead and inspire the others. I then set about finding a planning process that would work for us.

I met Verne Harnish, the author of *Mastering the Rockefeller Habits*, several years ago. He has a very nifty way of doing a plan and the planning process with everything tied up on one single (big) page. I liked the way it provided us with a framework, so that together with the team leaders we could assess, judge and ultimately choose what actions we needed to take to move forward. Its structure allows for five main focuses or objectives for the period (we use trimesters). Once the company top five are set, it then translates into a top five for each team and then a top five for each individual. This means that everyone's top fives are aligned to reach the same destination.

'When you think about something it is a dream, when you envision it, it's exciting. When you plan it, it's possible. But when you do it, it's real!"
Anthony Robbins

Another revelation to me after meeting Verne was the concept of setting a 'rhythm' within your organisation.

Have you ever had that infectious feeling when you just cannot stop your feet from tapping, or you just cannot get a song out of your head? I used to be a runner, and anytime

i want what she's having

I was particularly challenged by the incline or the sheer distance I would revert to a different state – counting. I often felt I could run forever as long as I was in a rhythm. I had no mental consciousness of anything else. My friend Sarah, who is a Yoga instructor, said that it was probably my equivalent of a meditative state. One foot would just keep going out in front the other, following. No thought was needed. No planning, no discussion, no debate, no analysis; the rhythm was what caused me to run.

Isn't it the same with business? When it is in a rhythm things just seem to happen by themselves. The tough bit is setting off. The first kilometre is the hardest in any run, relaxing, getting your stride. And I think it is the same in a business. But setting the rhythm in place, even when you are tiny, sets up how it will go when you are bigger. This is just the way we do things around here. No reinventing the wheel over and over again.

But let me take it back a step. In working in various large organisations, one of the big gripes I would hear is "I have no idea what is going on here" or "No one tells us anything" or "I hear there is some new program being launched but I don't know the details" etc.

If we have gone to all the effort of producing a plan, what is the point if we are not delivering on it? Success is 98 percent about the execution of the plan. And the only way you know where the plan is up to is by focusing on it – all the time.

"A good plan violently executed today is far and away better than a perfect plan tomorrow." General George S. Patton

When I was at Apple, I had an amazing manager – well, I had many – but the first manager I had was fantastic. And I tried to identify exactly what it was that she did that made me as an employee feel so great.

It was really simple – I was heard. I had a weekly scheduled one-on-one with her. I knew when it was, I looked forward to it and I planned for it.

So I said to myself, I will have one-on-ones with everyone in my company, this will make sure I stay in touch with what is going on and what customers and suppliers are saying. Great with seven employees, but at 15 it became unwieldy, let alone at 40 and beyond.

What do other organisations do? As founder I love being involved in everything but then I become a stopping point. Then when I heard someone mumble to another 'I never know what is going on around here', I thought I've got to do something to make the way we communicate flexible enough to evolve no matter how big we grow.

Inspired in part by *Mastering the Rockefeller Habits*, I set up a communication rhythm that ensured everyone in the organisation knew what was going on and how we were going with achieving the plan.

We have two weekly team leader meetings, an extended one and a short one. Both meetings are designed with a specific agenda. We share what is working, and what's not working (the stop points that prevent us from meeting the plan). Sometimes stop points can be quickly dealt with here, other times they might have to be taken out of the meeting for resolution 'off line'.

Each team leader then meets with their direct reports for 10 minutes to download what they just learned and they then follow the same process to find out if there are any stop points which are preventing their team members from achieving their top fives.

I have a weekly scheduled one-on-one with each of the team leaders, and they have one-on-ones with each of their people. This is primarily a coaching session, finding out what is happening, seeking input, and seeing if I can support them in any way. I look forward to these. I have five team leaders so there's one meeting a day. I keep notes of what I want to discuss with each of them, so I don't keep interrupting them all day with emails or questions.

Knowing when you are meeting means that you save time and are much more productive but it does take practice and discipline to put things in a parking lot until the next day.

But wait – there are more meetings! There are monthly company meetings where we get together over lunch to share the successes of the past month, create the next month and recognise the 'stars' of the month. The idea behind these meetings is to create connectedness and acknowledge contribution from individuals in front of their peers. Finally we have our trimester planning sessions, reviews and creativity cook-ups.

Every one of these meetings is documented, has an agenda and a clear purpose. Together with our internal blog, wiki and now podcasts of important meetings, I can put my hand on my heart and say if a RedBallooner does not know what is going on then they're not living our values. The point is that by nature the team loves to be in the know, and all of our communication tools allow them to find out quickly and precisely what's going on.

The good thing about setting a rhythm now is that this model will work when the company grows.

The rhythm has set us free. We don't waste time trying to find a time in each others' diaries, we spend the rest of the time outwardly focused. It might sound busy, but you would expect a fast-growing business to be busy – the point is that it is not chaotic.

We struggled for four years doing annual plans broken into quarterly activities. (A year is a very long time in a fast-growing business's life). Some years we guessed low and everyone was happy, some years we guessed high and there were tears. The point is that they are just guesses, based on not very much history. We were so attached to the numbers.

The other thing with our planning was that a quarter was way to short to do anything other than tactical activities, and a year took forever. With the seasonality of our business all effort went into quarter two and quarter three was very much the unloved child.

I have been looking for the book of business rules which says that to have a successful business you must divide your planning and reporting into quarters (I have no analysts or shareholders to report to so I'm not bound by such restrictions. If you find the book of rules let me know because we have clearly broken this planning rule. But it is really working. With a quarter too short and a year too long, we chose three trimesters each lasting four months. Each trimester is long enough to do some real work and is not dependent on seasonal fluctuations – December and January are both snugly in Trimester Two. This reduces the number of plans we do in a year by 25 percent.

It's about creating the rules for your game that suit your business, not playing to someone else's tune.

i want what she's having

The serious side to the game

Even if your organisation is running like clockwork, if you've neglected the financial side of the business, then no amount of efficient regular communication will sort things out. Chris Jones, presenter of Westpac's *Beyond Survival* program believes there are seven common causes of under-performing businesses: failure to plan, to monitor finances, to understand the relationship between price, volume and costs, to manage cash flow, to manage growth, to borrow properly and plan for transition (exit).

I won't go into detail about each of the points in the above list, suffice to say that you've got to have your business finances sorted, otherwise the bigger you get, the harder it all becomes to implement. We often use the points above as a checklist to keep ourselves on track, regularly asking ourselves which ones we are managing well and which ones we are neglecting.

Each business uses its own particular metrics to keep tabs on how they are faring. It might be profit per employee, billable hours, stock holding time, number of customers in a queue or number of hits to a website. At RedBalloon our critical number is "How many days out did we sell today?" which is closely tied to our BHAG. We focus on the number of people to whom we gave a good time (while keeping a very close eye on the money in the bank too!).

Finding a number that is relevant, that means something to everyone and that supports the business fiscally pulls the team towards one goal. The great thing about being in the online world is that we track everything and we can count anything. This collated information becomes a very powerful tool for us to compare our performance week on week, year on year and to continually improve.

Without the financial means, you can't make the difference that you want to. A business has to be profitable. I want my suppliers to be profitable otherwise they won't be there for my customers. It is not a successful business unless it is profitable enough to be able to continually innovate.

Profits and cash are not related so it is important for us to understand the working capital cycle, which means ensuring that we get paid quickly. When I ran Bright Marketing, one of the things I hated the most was chasing invoices. I'd deliver the service, pay the contractors and service providers then wait to be paid. I had made a profit on paper but had nothing in the bank. I know there is debtor financing and all that, but really – I'd delivered the service and I just wanted to be paid. You can fall out of love with a client pretty quickly if they don't pay. Some of them were essentially saying to me "I want the service now and we'll pay you in six months." There's no integrity in that and I don't like doing business that way.

So I established a condition that my clients had to pay fifty percent of the fees on appointment, and that work on a client's project would not commence until these funds were received. The invoicing was easy; it was the receipt of payment that took the time. If they really wanted you to do the work and you didn't start until you saw the money, then any problems with becoming a preferred supplier were sorted out really quickly.

I know how I hated being treated as a supplier at Bright Marketing, and it's shaped how I now treat our RedBalloon suppliers. We pay our suppliers in advance before the participant arrives at their experience. It is one of the things that I'm most proud of in this business. People love being paid in advance and the result is that I have hundreds of suppliers who deliver the RedBalloon promise. Paying them in advance means that they can get on with what they are great at – delivering pleasure – and not worry about the money. They might even tell other people what a great organisation we are to do business with!

I cannot stress enough the importance of borrowing properly and having a great relationship with your financial people including accountants, advisors and bankers. We see our Westpac banker, Paul, as an extension of our business. He knows what we are up to and what we are trying to do. He is really committed to the success of our business, and as such keeps streamlining our financial facilities and borrowings to match us as we grow. Financial support for employees is important too and Brett, who looks after the superannuation of our staff, is as passionate about our business as we are.

I'll share a lovely story with you to highlight the importance of these financial relationships. A few years ago we had a woman call our Pleasure Relations team, and she delivered the following brief: "My mother in law is turning eighty; she has everything and is quite hard to please. Have you any ideas?" My team put together two experiences to create a special day, arranging a personal dinner party on

Sydney Harbour's North Head with her immediate family, and a butterfly release ceremony – one butterfly for each year of her life. We heard later that she had tears in her eyes as she watched the butterflies. "I don't cry for the years that have flown but for the lives that I've given," she whispered.

Many months later I was speaking to our banker who said, "Oh by the way, thanks so much for doing my mother's 80th birthday. It was absolutely delightful." We had no idea that our 80th birthday girl was our banker's mother! Our bank knows the business that we are in.

While business is very much a game with a unique set of rules which provide a steady operational rhythm, there is a serious financial side to doing business which must be constantly monitored. Find your critical number and keep it 'in the face' of every employee so you are all heading in the one positive direction.

Displaying the RedBalloon critical numbers has been an easy task, thanks to the adoption of certain cutting-edge technology and reporting programs. Never shying away from an opportunity to be entrepreneurial and to remain ahead of the game, we have a propensity to seek out the latest technologies to make our lives easier.

8

chapter 8
Savvy And Proud Of It

At RedBalloon such is our dedication to embracing new technologies, ideas and programs, I can say with no hesitation that if it moves, we can normally measure it and if it's a repetitive process that makes our jobs dull and unexciting, we can normally find a way to automate it.

I've known people that have done the same job for years, who have followed inefficient processes set up for them by their predecessors and who have never questioned them. At RedBalloon I want people to evolve and to take pride in their work, to discover and learn new things. Administration is a necessity, but it shouldn't be all-consuming and so I actively encourage my people to think of ways to improve the efficiencies in their individual roles. I ask them to think "Is this a good use of my time? Am I moving the game forward by doing this?"

Often we do things because we have always done it that way, not because it's the most efficient way to do it. We've saved considerable man hours over the years just by using technology to tell us what we need to know.

We have used open source software, created our own systems and now we have a unique mixture that allows anyone in the organisation to find out what's going on at any time.

I truly believe that one of the reasons RedBalloon is and continues to be so successful is because of our eagerness to try and experiment with new forms of technology we think would increase efficiency.

I spoke in the last chapter about critical numbers and keeping them in the face of every employee. Well clearly a messy whiteboard in a meeting room where only a few employees go is not going to cut it. So we use technology to ensure that everyone has an opportunity to see the scoreboard everyday. Every time a RedBallooner logs in, they have an opportunity to see how we are going in real time, as our little scoreboard bar chart appears and begins racing up the screen. It's hilarious too, as sometimes when we are only 10 or so experience vouchers away from a particular goal, some people will literally sit on the scoreboard and continually press refresh, so that they can be the first person to shout that we've made it!

Another thing that's great about the way we use technology is that we have cut the number of group emails we send to practically zero by introducing our own internal blog. Blogs have been around for a number of years, but seem to have become a lot more prolific during the last 12 months. We introduced ours about 15 months ago and it has become the landing page for everyone in the organisation. Every morning, we eagerly logon to read the new postings, whether it be to view pictures of an event, to tell us about a new campaign or a simple housekeeping announcement. And it's great for those who have been on annual leave, as they can find out what they've missed simply by logging on. We podcast our monthly meetings for this very reason too.

I also write my own blog naomisimson.com.au in the public domain to share what I learn from the multitude of people I meet, books I read or things I hear. My blog aims to transparently share what it's really like to run a fast growing business. I document freely the frustrations I come up against, reasons for celebration and I link to other blogs that I find inspiring or useful. I hope that by sharing this information I can assist and inspire others wherever they may be in the blogosphere.

AT REDBALLOON I WANT PEOPLE
TO EVOLVE AND TO TAKE
PRIDE IN THEIR WORK,
TO DISCOVER AND LEARN NEW
THINGS.

But our love of technology doesn't stop there. Another form of technology we have appropriated for our own means and that we are very proud is our wiki. The word 'wiki' most people will recognise from the popular free online encyclopedia en.wikipedia.org. The main difference between a wiki and a standard encyclopedia is that the wikipedia is collaborative, meaning that people can add to its contents. The way we have appropriated the wiki software is essentially to make a mini encyclopedia of RedBalloon that any RedBalloon employee can input into. It's great because emails containing ridiculously long file paths that you could never remember and therefore never bothered to look at became obsolete.

Look familiar?
To access the August 2006 report please go to:
V:\RedBalloon\RedBalloon 2006\Strategy\Finance\
Reports\Details\Spreadsheets\Quarter2\June\
AugustReport.xls

We put the facts on wiki for our people to see and links of where they can go internally for more information. The wiki has become our induction process for new starters. Literally everything they need to know can be found there and everything a RedBallooner anywhere needs can be accessed to ensure they stay in touch.

Using technology like this means that there is actually no need (apart from our Pleasure Relations team) for anyone to be in the office! Of course we all want to be there because that's where all the fun stuff happens, but technology has set us free and allowed us to be flexible. So we do offer, where applicable, the opportunity for some of our people to work from home one day a week. Also it's great when someone has a horrible cold, but doesn't want to take a sick day – we just say "go and work from home and keep your germs to yourself!" (It's amazing how quickly germs spread in offices!)

I know I annoy everyone in the office when I'm travelling on business because with my trusty Next G card I am never out of touch. I find airports so boring that I can't help myself and I go and find a quiet spot to email off a few ideas here and there. However, there is a flipside to being this well connected – it can make you a little bit obsessive. Just one more email or one more look at the scoreboard will often keep me up past midnight. I used to have one of those Palm Treo things, but I never could get it working properly! I just couldn't stop looking at it and it never stopped beeping, so I went back to a normal mobile phone and now just ensure my Mac never leaves my side.

But back to the technology – everything I have talked about so far is what we use to keep us in the loop and ensure no-one ever misses out, but we also use technology to help us do our own jobs. Whether it's a new project planning tool, a new way of logging website bugs or a new report that we can create that removes endless spreadsheets.

I have a great example where technology replaced what would be a particularly laborious process. We had created a corporate marketing tool called the Little Red Book of Answers (literally a little red book containing answers to questions on employee happiness, reward and recognition and more), and we decided to do our first ever corporate marketing campaign to promote this. We planned to mail out tens of thousands of postcards asking people whether they would like a copy of the Little Red Book. Of interest to us, of course, was who had requested the book, where they were from and where they would like their book delivered. However, the RedBalloon team members assigned to dispatch and follow up on the book were completely different. We also had two databases, one that was more for our consumer customers where the online request form would deposit the information and another Sugar CRM system to record correspondence with our corporate customers. I could sense this becoming another spreadsheet process unless I did something, so I stepped in and asked how hard it would be to get these two distinctly different databases to talk to each other. Of course it took energy and effort, but what I found was it was possible.

As Little Red Book requests came flooding in, emails were sent to one person for dispatch and simultaneously the details were copied to our Sugar system. Then, at the same time, a reminder containing the requestor's contact details was set to flash up six weeks from the requested date in the task list of one of the business development team. All they had to do was pick up the phone and say "Did you get your Little Red Book? Did you like it? Can we assist you in any way?" The leads flowed in and the sales ensued but how much harder would it have been had the whole process not been automated? I'm sure other businesses could have done all this standing on their heads. But for us it was an exciting moment.

And of course it made me want to automate everything. Much of this we have developed ourselves. Many of the solutions that have been relatively easy to integrate into our world are out there inexpensively in the open source world.

chapter 9
Get People Talking

I don't know about you but I find that if something amazing happens to me, or I find a fabulous new product on the market or a new way of doing something, then I can't wait to tell lots of people about it. I'll ring my husband and tell him about a fantastic new car I've seen or I'll ring my girlfriends and tell them about a delicious new restaurant I've eaten at on the weekend. I share my discoveries and my experiences, spreading the word about what I've done or where I've been. So it comes as no surprise that I try to inspire the same reaction in my customers – the people who experience RedBalloon in its entirety. How do I generate the same level of excitement and enthusiasm that will render people unable to resist ringing someone and telling them about RedBalloon?

If you want people to spread the word about your business to their friends, work colleagues, family and others, you've got to give them something worth talking about. You've got to give them a story that they can share with others, embellish, give a personal touch to, and capture the attention of others. I'll share with you a great anecdote that helps illustrate this point.

One of the first events Sol Trujillo ever attended as the new CEO for Telstra was the 2005 Telstra Business Awards at which RedBalloon was present. A few months later I was asked to attend an intimate session of about 20 people with Sol. I was the only woman there. Sol wanted to listen particularly to three key feedback areas from each attendee – what business were we in, what innovative things did we have on the go, and what part did we see Telstra playing in that?

We took turns contributing and I was amazed at some of the things Australian businesses were getting up to. There was someone who was finding water in the desert, another who was doing lifesaving surgery over the internet. I sat there truly humbled by the greatness of Australian innovation, wondering what I would say.

About half-way through the group it was my turn. "Hello my name is Naomi Simson from RedBalloon Days … and we give great pleasure," I said. There were looks of shock and disbelief and no-one knew where to look! I'm sure they were thinking, "How did 'she' get in here?" What would they tell their wives when they got home?

I continued, "I'm the Chief Experience Officer and this year we will deliver 40,000 great experiences." I went on to share the difference RedBalloon has made to hundreds of businesses, my passion for employee engagement and of course, my experiences with Telstra.

Everyone who was present in the room that day will never forget what RedBalloon Days does. I shocked them and cheekily gave them something worth remembering, and hopefully worth passing on to others.

Knock your socks off experiences

Ask yourself: "What is truly remarkable about what I give my customers? Is it an amazing or different product or service? Would they be inspired to tell their friends about it?" Good enough is not enough to inspire someone to tell others about their experience with your organisation. You've got to give them a 'knock your socks off' experience, so they

103

won't be able to resist telling someone about it. You must wow them.

I received this email from someone in our 'shop' (our online store):

"Hi, I haven't YET done anything on your website ... but I just found it about 20 minutes ago and I haven't been able to take my eyes off it. I love it! I have sent the website address to everyone in my contacts list and called half of the people and surfed the site with them. I plan on working my way through a lot of the things on offer over the next few months Thank you so much for offering all of these packages and opportunities! I love it! :)" Danielle

She is so delighted, to the point where she has been compelled to contact her friends to share the excitement of her find. This is fantastic for helping build our brand awareness. But this is just the start of our relationship with this woman. Once her immediate attention has been captured, how can I knock her socks off and continue to wow her with a completely positive experience with our brand? She is still a potential customer, and we have to impress her at every step along the way – through her web searching, providing enticing images, making the website user friendly, in order to turn her into a paying customer. And it doesn't stop there. We must ensure that every piece of contact that Danielle has with RedBalloon is amazing.

This is easier than it sounds, particularly since we are an online business, with the majority of our transactions being done on the internet. It's impersonal and there is little direct personal contact with our customers. We can't look them in the eye, build any level of report, use empathy or tap into their emotions face-to-face. The biggest question we face is, "How can we delight you if we're not there in person?"

Our corporate customer relationships tend to have more personal interaction, but our general consumer relationships lack that human touch. Yet these consumers and potential consumers are the keepers of the stories that will determine RedBalloon's future. How can we possibly build a level of rapport with them? We haven't got the perfect answer yet, but we're always implementing tactics that let our personality shine through, in our email messages, in all of our website copy, in our personalised e-newsletters, in our phone conversations and in our personalised reviews and images of ourselves doing experiences on the site.

And of course we now put our direct contact details info on the base of all of our emails so that we're only one point of contact away from them if they need to speak to someone.

Getting people to share your story

What do you have to do to ensure the word will travel? Amaze your customers by doing what you say you're going to do on time or ahead of time – consistently. Delight them by meeting and exceeding their expectations if you can, by daring to be different and by constantly innovating to keep things fresh.

One of the great things about doing what I do is that whenever I travel on business or with the family I am always on the hunt for some unknown experiences. You can

i want what she's having

find them anywhere; chatting to your brother-in-law, to a coffee shop owner, but not usually to the tourists – they are too obvious. I got chatting with the surf shop owner at Prevelly Beach in WA's Margaret River when I was there on a family holiday, to find out what was going on in this little corner of the world. He cautioned not to swim at the beach because a shark named Bruce had taken up residency, and he told me about local world champion kite surfers, quad biking and night walks near Prevelly Beach. Regarding the best places to get a feed, he said, "Well I hear that the place next door is really quite good. In fact a man was telling me that they have world class duck". "Ooh," I thought "I love duck." We had friends coming down from Perth that night to join us for dinner and I told them about this world class duck.

When we arrived at the restaurant, guess who was sitting at the bar? The surf shop owner. I quickly wanted to set the record straight with my dinner companions: "You know how I said this restaurant has world class duck? Well it might not, because the guy who told me about it is sitting right there and he is probably on the payroll getting kickbacks for referring tourists." So no one orders the duck, except me. Out comes the duck, and it is melt-in-your-mouth, crispy, golden, drop-off-the bone world class duck. The only bad thing about the duck was that I had to share it with everyone else at the table! Because of my positive experience, I have told so many people about that amazing duck, and with only one restaurant in Prevelly Beach, there is no mistaking where to go.

Conversely, if this experience had not met my expectations, I may have spoken badly about it to others or just not said anything at all. I would not have continued spreading the word about this restaurant. If an experience does not meet people's expectations, that is, what they were told by someone else or what they were promised, then they will stop talking about it. At RedBalloon, we know we only get one chance to impress our customers enough to spread the story about their experience to others. It must be right the first time.

Little things can make all the difference

Everyone can make a difference and create meaningful memories for customers that will motivate them to come back to your company and tell other people about how delighted they were. Even something as simple as putting a personal signature on a letter or letting your personality shine through on a phone call can make all the difference. Small actions speak volumes.

There's a little book called 'The Simple Truths of Service – Inspired by Johnny the Bagger' by Ken Blanchard and Barbara Glanz, which offers an inspiring message about giving something extra and unexpected to your customers to make them feel special; a memory that will make them want to come back or tell a friend. It's such a simple idea but it's so powerful and I encourage you to read this book and to think about a small action you can implement that will impact the customer experience.

Since leaving corporate life I have often reflected on why many people leave their personality at the door when they arrive at work. Is it a desire to fit the 'company mould' by morphing into the company's projected ideal personality, in order to avoid being the odd one out? Or perhaps it's a

i want what she's having

reflection of a tightly controlled company environment that does not support its employees being individuals and using their unique strengths and talents. Whatever the reason, I think it's a great shame if employees do not feel able to be themselves at work, to personalise their desk, to let their warmth and humanity come through.

Our RedBalloon team members regularly go off to sample the experiences of our suppliers. They return with photos or DVDs in hand, write a review on how the day went and we publish it on the website. We're very transparent about who we are, and take pleasure in sharing our personalities with our third parties, letting people 'in'. We have fun doing these experiences and we want people to see us having fun so we can inspire them with our own stories. Our Pleasure Relations team members sometimes even stick a photo of themselves doing a great experience at the bottom of their emails and have a link to their personalised review! Our customers have given us great feedback about this simple action – they love seeing what we look like, and feel that they can get to know us by seeing what we love to do and what we are passionate about. We give them something worth reading and worth talking about.

It's OK to let your personality shine, lighten up and have fun. It doesn't always have to be serious. If your staff leave their personality at home and are not encouraged to let their true character emerge at work, I guarantee that they won't put much energy and enthusiasm into providing 'knock your socks off' service to your customers.

Having said this, I don't believe that you can coerce your staff into being amazing all the time, and delivering great service all the time. They either love people or they don't.

They either want to make a difference or they don't. They either care or they don't. This comes back to the individual's values and strengths. Ultimately everyone makes a choice. Are they going to have a good time that day or not? It is up to them.

People tellers – creating an epidemic

Back in 1987 I found myself in a milk bar in Darwin with my friend Christina, with whom I had been travelling overland from Denmark. She asked the milk bar owner for a bottle of water. He responded "We have two kinds – orange and passionfruit or orange and mango." We had just travelled through China (only a decade or so after the Cultural Revolution) where bottled drinking water, green tea and bottled coke were all that we would drink.

Christina said, "I just want plain mineral water," so the milk bar owner returned with a blue can. "No, just plain water – no bubbles," she said. The owner look at her puzzled, "But why would you want that? Plain water comes from the tap!"

Jumping forward to 2007, 25 per cent of all Australians and New Zealanders regularly put bottled water in their shopping trolleys. Why such a big change? Was it all the great advertising that people have seen for bottled water? I can't recall one.

What happened here was that someone thought it was a good idea to buy water in bottles, they told other people who also thought it was a good idea and started buying bottled water, and the idea took hold quickly. A water epidemic was created. If you have read Malcom Gladwell's book *The Tipping Point* you will know that there are different types of 'people tellers' and know what causes an epidemic. Imagine if you could harness such an epidemic where people are so busy talking about you, spreading the word about your concept, that you don't need to advertise.

We all want to keep up with the Jones's. Remember that scene in *When Harry met Sally?* – "I want what she's having." When we hear a great story about a movie, restaurant or book we'll give it a try. But if it is not what we expected, our conversation about it will stop.

When you delight people, that is, deliver them something that completely meets their expectations or something that is totally unexpected, then hopefully they will return the favour by delighting you by telling others about their experience. It starts with a vision, put into action, other people will buy into your vision and the word will travel.

'WE ENJOY TALKING ABOUT OUR
EXPERIENCES MUCH MORE THAN
OUR PESSESSIONS.
TALKING ABOUT OUR EXPERIENCES
– INCLUDING OUR SHARED
EXPERIENCES
IS THE STOCK IN TRADE OF OUR RELATIONSHIPS...
GOOD RELATIONSHIPS ARE
STRONGLY ASSOCIATED WITH
HAPPINESS

GEFFINSER
FEBRUARY 18 2004
ACTIVITY IS THE GOODS FOR TRUE SATISFACTION
THE SYDNEY MORNING HERALD

chapter 10
Building The Brand –
On A Shoe-String
Budget

Nurturing relationships

I was visiting a RedBalloon customer in Melbourne, now the CEO of a large publicly-listed company, and he seemed very familiar. He thought I looked familiar as well. It finally clicked that 18 years earlier we had both been participants on the Golden Wing Board of Advisors at Ansett. He said, "You know in those days I would have been on an Ansett aircraft five days out of seven. I somehow felt that I owned it, that it was mine. I definitely felt I was part of the business. So when I was appointed to the advisory panel it didn't just validate how I felt about the airline, it gave me authority to continue to speak about it to anyone who would listen."

What this initiative of Ansett's did was to move a loyal customer beyond advocacy to being an integral part of the brand.

Many groups of people make up the RedBalloon brand. Our employees, the customers who purchase from us, the recipients of our gift vouchers who actually have the experiences, the suppliers who are contracted to us and the companies who choose to deal with us are also our brand. All these groups are part of the RedBalloon story and they help us spread the story to others, enticing others to form a relationship with our brand.

"Hi there, I organised a gift voucher for my Uncle & Aunty through RedBalloon as a Christmas present last year which consisted of a scenic flight over Sydney and the North and

South Shores. My Uncle and Aunty, Sue and Bill Hutton, took this flight on Sunday June 4th. RedBalloon handed over to the supplier to fulfil the experience, and Sue and Bill have informed me that the day and the service provided was nothing short of exceptional. I'd like to thank Megan and the wonderful team for the way in which my Uncle and Aunty were looked after! The organisation and communication leading up to the event I'm told was meticulous and very accommodating and thoughtful to their location on the Central Coast. There is always the element of the unknown with giving vouchers such as these to family and friends but when I heard of the way in which the company treated their guests I was very impressed and will have no hesitation in giving gift vouchers and organising events through RedBalloon in the future. Thank you once again for offering such a great service and for just being genuinely nice people." David Crumpton

People feel connected to a brand because they have relationships with people within that brand. A RedBalloon experience participant is connected to other RedBalloon participants by virtue of sharing and comparing their experiences with each other, they are connected to the suppliers who have delivered their experience, and they are connected to the person who gave them the experience. Brand equity is created in absolutely every relationship and every dealing that RedBalloon has with others.

i want what she's having

It's all well and good to have brand equity in the form of strong relationships within, and external to, an organisation, but I believe a finer measure of people's connectedness to a brand is the level of brand intimacy that exists. I'm talking about a sense of true relatedness which causes these people to respond to, defend, contribute to and advocate that brand. We have to constantly amaze and delight our customers to build a greater level of intimacy.

I lived in New York in the mid 1980s when Coca-Cola decided to launch 'New Coke'. They changed the recipe, the formula, and released a new potion. The outcry was deafening and news reports, CNN and MTV all ran major articles and it was on the front page of US Today. It was not very long before Coca-Cola had to make a public retraction. But it was several months before 'Classic Coke' was able to be launched. The general population believed that they owned the Coke brand and they literally took to the streets when the company did not do what they thought was the right thing for the brand. Imagine reaching this level of brand intimacy with your customers that would cause them to react like this?!

Delivering on our brand promise

We all like dealing with the people we like and tend to avoid doing business with those that we don't. To ensure RedBalloon is one of the businesses that others want to have a relationship with, it's essential that we consistently fulfill on our promise to do what we say we are going to do.

An acquaintance once remarked how much he loved the RedBalloon website. I said, "Thanks. Do you use us yourself personally or is it for business use – corporate gifting or for recognising your staff?" "Well no," he answered a bit sheepishly. Of course I pressed on, "So you like what we do but you don't buy." He answered, "Well it is a fantastic directory service. It gives us great ideas and then we see if we can track down a similar experience and book direct." I was flabbergasted. "But why wouldn't you use our service which offers recourse if something happens and where the experiences are tested by many before you? All experiences are not equal you know. We only choose the ones that meet our guidelines."

He said, "Basically we are stingy and every penny counts in our business." I told him that on the RedBalloon website you pay exactly the same price for an experience as if you went direct to the supplier. He said he didn't realise that and offered a key observation … "Perhaps you could let your visitors know. We had the idea that you were expensive."

Thanks to this (now) friend we invented our 100 percent Pleasure Guarantee which is a bold commitment to "Give you 100 percent of your money back if you find that the supplier has a cheaper price." To make this guarantee a true promise we put our money where our mouth is. If we had said that we would pay the difference between our price and the supplier price, it's not a big enough deal. $5 here or there is not enough to really drive us and our supply partners to integrity. A brand promise has to be strong enough that if you fail to fulfil on it, it is painful. So we agreed that the full payment of any price discrepancies must be made out of our precious marketing budget which is agony, but it keeps us focused on fulfilling our promise and proves that we are committed.

i want what she's having

If you are going to make a brand promise it better be bold. FedEx's 'When it's absolutely got to be there' sticks and is worth talking about.

I was still concerned about my friend's observation that RedBalloon experiences appeared expensive. We charge exactly the same as our suppliers so why would we be perceived as expensive? If you are comparing us to a book, DVD or similar gift, then an experience will be perceived as a more expensive gift. The fact is that experiences involve people as well as insurance, possibly fuel and lots of overheads; all unavoidable costs. We are never going to be a cheap gift option, so we will never be in the business of competing on price. We prefer to engage in value-based conversations with customers, knowing that people like to feel that they have received value for money.

Dialogue vs monologue

Brand equity is created throughout every experience that others have with that brand. Organisations that allow others to take part in creating them, adding to them and evolving them via two-way feedback and contributions will increase the level of intimacy between the third party and the brand. Establishing an environment of open communication with our customers is one way that we invite them to directly influence our product and our organisation itself. These days, people want a dialogue, not a monologue. The online sphere provides an easy medium for such communication, and is largely self-managed by the participants. MySpace.com, del.ic.ious, flickr.com and Wikipedia are good examples of online communities based on connectedness and open two-way communication.

I asked the managing director of eBay Australia what has contributed to their success. He said it is due to the fact that they created an online environment where customers have the power to determine the quality of what is being sold. It is the eBay customers that keep other customers honest. Customers rating other merchant customers is a fairly transparent practice. It is the customers that uphold the brand promise.

But can a bricks and mortar organisation offer a reasonable level of open two-way communication? It's possible, but requires a great deal of manual effort to collate the feedback, respond to each one, keep contributors informed of the status of their proposed ideas and discuss potential innovations if it is to become a successful two-way relationship. Customers want to hear back from us, otherwise they will feel that their idea has just disappeared into the ether. I remember speaking with a woman from a large department store. She said that they had suggestion boxes for customers in every store but she admitted that not only did she not know what was suggested, she had no idea if they were ever read, let alone put into action. She thought it very unlikely that the person who made a suggestion ever found out what happened to their idea, regardless of whether the idea became a reality. The department store had set up a one-way monologue, rather than a dialogue, which is what customers are demanding. One-way communications do little to build the relationship between customers and a brand.

i want what she's having

Listening well can add value

Young marketers often ask me what they can do to get ahead in their career. I tell them by understanding the customer experience – get close to them, ask them questions, listen to them, watch how they react, understand what is important to them, learn how they want to do business with you. A thousand customers means a thousand opportunities to learn. It takes time.

We know that communication is not about what is said but what is listened. We hear words but we have to listen for meaning. So it is one thing to get people talking, but how do you get people to listen?

I remember as a young child my art teacher drumming into me the definition of communication. It is not whether the word was spoken or not, it was not even whether it was heard. It was only if the word was listened to and became knowledge that it could be called communication.

I think of those that I listen to; mentors, educators and business leaders to name a few. What is it that makes me really listen to them? I know that I have a certain way of always listening for 'gold' but it is more than that. I can be listening to a speaker, think that that person is incredibly gifted, talented and generous, only to discover that others in the same group were not impressed at all. Clearly something was missing for them.

Good communicators possess two key qualities – empathy and a sense of relatedness. They also have something worth saying, too.

For me, empathy is not how someone would react to a situation in another's shoes. Rather, it is being able to experience life in that person's shoes, really being in their world. If you are speaking to a group of graduates you have to remember what it was like not to know if you would land a job, being totally idealistic about the world of employment, wanting to travel and to have it all. Your approach needs to be tailored to each audience to maximise the chance of them engaging with you and really listening to you. For some people, empathy is a natural strength, whereas others really have to work hard at it.

Relatedness means working out who is there to listen to you, why they are there and what they want to get out of it. As the speaker, you are there for them – not for yourself. Some of the most generous speakers I have heard such as Gail Kelly, Malcom Turnbull and Tim Pethick really give of themselves; they allow themselves to be vulnerable and they quickly establish how they relate to their audience, how they are the same, how ordinary they are to whomever they are speaking. Because they don't pitch themselves as 'better than you', a sense of relatedness is created and you instantly listen.

The same principles apply for one-on-one conversations or interaction within small groups.

I know that if I have several points that I really need to get across, one of the first things I do is plan. This does not mean wordsmith and rote learning, but simply anticipating

i want what she's having

where I want the conversation to go. I want to be able to guide the conversation without controlling it. I've also learned that in business, and in life, I have to have the toughest conversations as soon as possible. They are never as bad as you think they are going to be and putting them off only distracts you from the task at hand. Simply by being authentic and totally straight with your audience, being in their world and trying to relate to them, can make all the difference to helping someone listen to you.

You never know who is going to say what when, so listening carefully can add phenomenal value to your business.

Sometimes customers will have an insight or suggestion that will ultimately determine your strategy. We're constantly listening to our customers and potential customers to hear what they are saying to us, via organised feedback channels. About 14 per cent of experience participants respond to our 'How Was It For You?' feedback email after their experience. Our Pleasure Relations team responds to several hundred enquiry emails a week which come through the 'Contact Us' section on the website and also from automatically generated emails. Overall, RedBalloon sends out thousands of emails a day, both personal and auto-generated.

The ability to listen well is so important. Do you remember playing Chinese whispers at school? We played it at the office once, just for fun, and I discovered that my team are really good listeners. We did it partly because for the first time in the history of the universe I had lost my voice. What did we learn by playing this game? Everyone retained more of the message because they were forced to really listen.

I regularly put myself on the phones with the Pleasure Relations team, receiving calls from customers. What a fantastic experience it is and what a privilege to listen to our customers first hand. I find this a much more valuable exercise than conducting a market research survey from time to time to find out what your customers are saying. Each time I'm on the phones I learn so much, and I'll share some of my findings with you without any judgement or laying blame on anyone. It is just how it is:

- People don't read. Why should they? If you are running a website then it must be absolutely evident what the customer is getting and what is expected of them. It has to be more than obvious. It must be 'in your face', with no subtleties.
- Business is a people sport. Many people just want to speak to people, to find out if there are real people behind the website, what it's all about and how it works. You think, let's have a chat anyway. Sometimes it is just nice to shoot the breeze – you might just make the person's day.
- Simplicity wins every time. You can try to invent a system for everything. But the reality is that if you are dealing with 1,000 people there will be 1,000 different views of the world. Sometimes you just have to bend your knees and be flexible. Just because one person asks for something one way does not mean you need to invent a system to accommodate every variation.
- People will live into the game you create for them. Ultimately people love a challenge, they love to feel a sense of achievement. Not to be overwhelmed or under-resourced, just exhilarated by the sheer pleasure of

accomplishment. After all we all want to make a difference, and when we do, we feel fantastic.

We listened to our clients and launched in New Zealand!

Our move into New Zealand and the launch of GoDo was reliant on listening to our customers. A potential client had called me to discuss the potential of RedBalloon providing length of service awards for their company. They had been in business for more than 10 years and they wanted to celebrate this milestone. They wanted every experience delivered with a bunch of helium balloons on the anniversary of each person's employment. "No problems," I said, secretly petrified as I thought that they had added an extra zero to the estimated numbers by mistake! It was going to be a stretch for us to fulfil, but I tried to play it cool and not get excited. Then they asked "Do you have experiences in New Zealand?" "Ah, no, we don't now, but by Christmas we will have," I responded without hesitation.

New Zealand at that point was in no way on the agenda. We had only been around for two years and we were just beginning to make headway and we didn't want to get stretched too thin. But we won the account and as a woman of my word (calling in lots of favours!) we launched in New Zealand three months later.

After we had been in New Zealand for about eight months I went back to the client and said, 'Oh by the way, we're all set up in New Zealand now, so send through those length of service employee details to us and we will get the experiences all organised for you.' She responded casually 'Oh I think we have one person reaching their 10 year anniversary sometime next year.' I could have flown this employee first class to Sydney and given them any experience for less than the cost of setting up a whole new business.

Now there probably should have been a lesson in there about qualifying the size of the opportunity before you leap ahead of yourself, but that is not the lesson I learned. I learned that without being audacious, sometimes nothing will ever happen. New Zealand has been such a natural progression for our business and I'm glad we launched there when we did, even if it all happened hurriedly. Logic would have said, "Don't go to New Zealand at this time in your development," but we've found New Zealand to be a land of experience and both the suppliers and customers are a delight to deal with.

Listening to our customers and ensuring that they can get close enough to us to form a relationship with us, have been vital steps in building the RedBalloon brand. Their input has helped extend and improve our brand, and has been responsible for many innovations.

chapter 11
It's Not All About
The Big Ad

Advertising does not build brands – People build brands

Advertising is simply you talking about you, telling the world how fantastic you are. To help you communicate this message, you find a media partner who you believe will take your message beyond where you can get it by itself. That is what advertisers are in business to do and they are quite upfront about it; "We will create and run your ad, but we don't guarantee the result – that is up to you, the power of your advertisement and your ability to fulfil on its proposition."

After all my years in business I have realised that advertising is a waste of time, that it's absolutely hollow without a shred of integrity, unless you have a committed team around you who help fulfil the promise made by the piece. Integrity means doing what you say you're going to do – whole and complete work, no cutting corners, fulfilling completely on your word. A piece of advertising itself has no integrity; it is the committed team of employees who ensure that the product or service 'does what the ad says it will do' that provide the integrity to the message.

A great example to highlight the importance of integrity comes from Ansett around the time of deregulation of the airline industry in Australia. I was working for them at the time. The company decided to run a cultural change program in response to staff complaints that they were not kept informed of what was going on anymore, that they never saw the airline on TV and that life at Ansett was just not generally as good as it had been in the old days with Sir Reg.

In an attempt to rectify the situation, Ansett turned to the ad men rather than HR people and briefed their advertising agency. Back came a campaign called 'You can't have the greatest airline in the world without the greatest people'. A series of TV commercials were produced interviewing different groups of staff, from baggage handlers to pilots, catering staff to engineers. The campaign included print media, lots of signage at airports and badges for each employee. Even the placemats on the trays in the aircraft were emblazoned with the slogan!

My special role in this campaign was to produce a gift for each staff member, which needed to be personal and relevant. An aluminium baggage tag with leather strap was selected. Each had, 'You can't have the greatest airline in the world without the greatest people' on the reverse side, and the front of each tag was personally engraved with the person's name. This was before the days of digital technology and the engraver who got the job could not believe that he had just received an order for 12,000 engravings. It must have been his biggest order ever. I asked payroll for the names of all the people in the airline and also to find out where they were located so that I could arrange for the delivery of each of these items with a letter from the General Manager. What a mess. I had assumed that payroll would have the definitive list of who worked at the airline and where they lived. Not so. I used what information I had as best I could.

The complaints that came back were loud and clear: "You have always spelled my name wrongly and now it is

i want what she's having

even on my tag to prove it"; "She has not worked here for more than a year, she never came back from maternity leave'; "Where is mine? I've worked here for 12 years and you missed me" (as a contractor not on payroll); "What a waste of time and money".

The sentiment of the campaign was honourable, but the execution was a disaster and authenticity was clearly missing. By the time the engraver had finished, nearly six months had passed and 15,000 tags had been produced. I honestly thought that this was the last thing that I would ever do in my marketing career – fielding complaints from staff about how they were being treated by management. The problems extended throughout all facets of the airline. Badges with the slogan were on all front-line airline staff. For a customer whose bags did not arrive and who was possibly irate about several other things as well, to see a badge saying 'You can't have the greatest airline in the world without the greatest people' on the baggage claim clerk who is trying to explain to you that your luggage is not yet in the vicinity of the airport, is just hypocritical. The customer undoubtedly lets the baggage clerk know about their impression of this so called 'great airline' and what it can do with its 'great people'. The baggage clerk is not left feeling great, let alone powerfully being able to fulfil on his or her role. Morale declines instead of improves as the campaign intended.

To add insult to injury, this campaign was on air when the world's longest ever pilots' dispute began. The pilots chose to resign from the airlines (all of them) and there was no one left to fly the planes. Clearly something was missing if Ansett spent millions telling its own employees very publicly and expensively that they thought they were all great and yet during that campaign a vital percentage of those employees removed themselves from the game at hand.

Lesson learned: Slogans do not make a marketing campaign. If the customer experience did not meet what was promised then authenticity is missing.

Advertising has a place, but no one's listening

Advertising has a place, but not for making a sale. It is a post-sales activity used to reinforce the emotions that people feel about the brand, and to remind them of why they feel great when they deal with you. It should not be relied on to create relationships.

That's all well and good, but the issue that advertisers face is that consumers are so numb to advertising. On average we see thousands of messages a week and we simply cannot take it all in if it is just not relevant.

According to Eye Australia, who conducted a study in 2003, Australians are "increasingly unhappy with, and ignoring, advertising." In fact 81 percent of people say they are taking less notice of advertising. Most people find advertising boring and repetitive. We have become numb to the endless bombardment of 'promises'. And when the promise is not fulfilled by one organisation we become more cynical to all advertisers.

The majority of people say they are being bombarded with too much advertising and it "detracts from the experience of everyday life." It is so out of control in the

i want what she's having

US that according to Yankelovich Partners who did a study for the American Association of Advertisers, an alarming 33 percent of people surveyed would be willing to sacrifice their standard of living for a world without advertising!!

So if we don't pay attention to advertising who influences our purchase decisions? Gallup Organisation states that when it comes to who consumers trust it is 94 percent family and 87 percent friends. Only 27 percent trust the media, 23 percent corporations and 19 percent government.

If people tell their family and friends something they are going to listen in most instances.

I often ask people when I have public speaking engagements, "Do you remember seeing our great RedBalloon advertising campaign?" Every time I see blank faces. We have done so little advertising so the number one way that people have heard about us is from someone else.

So is advertising as we know it dead?

I'd argue that advertising is not dead – it is just transforming itself to meet the demands of the increasingly technology savvy and time-poor population. Advertising is becoming an on-request commodity; more personal, relevant and educational in order to communicate, build relationships and extend the story. I have high hopes for the future of marketing. But it will take a huge commitment to listening to customers and not being daunted by the big job at hand. The role of a marketer must change from being one who creates noise to one who listens and responds, as customers now want a dialogue not a monologue. Marketers must become quiet achievers.

Marketing communications are already changing from being directive ("This is what we are serving today so take it or leave it") to being influenced by the customers' own terms ("This is what I want to hear about and this is how I intend to learn about that information"). Consumers still want to learn about what is available to them, but they want the information where and when they want it, ensuring that it does not interrupt their entertainment consumption time.

The clever brands have tapped into this change and are throwing their marketing energies into creating pieces which consumers can access in their own space and time.

A good example is the viral email ads that have galloped around the globe, for instance the Carlton Draft 'very small ad' campaign, or the Axe Feather email which was sent to 30,000 people and ended up being opened by 52 million people who 'tickled' for an average of nine minutes. That has achieved broader reach than any TV ad audience in history, and it's unlikely that we would sit for nine minutes and watch a traditional TV commercial. So why would we do this for a viral email ad? Because we are engaged with the brand? (It's unlikely – the Axe viral ad was to launch a product that no one had ever heard of.) It is because we had the power of choice, we got to choose whether we read it or not, whether we wanted to play or not. We, the consumer, had the power.

By way of contrast, the everyday email and e-newsletter (wonderful communication tools before the influx of spam) are very much a push strategy. Even if you had people say that they wanted to hear from you, in the majority of cases we send emails based on what we want to say when we want to say it, rather than asking the receiver what they want to hear about, when they want to hear it and how they want to get those messages.

This is why more recent technology such as blogs and Real Simple Syndication (RSS feeds) are now so popular, because they allow the consumer to decide what they want to receive, when they receive it and they also get to interact with the sender.

Open communication methods are also proving popular, allowing customers to be involved in the marketing and idea-generation of a company. Since Mozilla released its open-source Firefox web browser software, more than 150 million users have downloaded it, which is not bad considering this non-profit foundation has no marketing staff to speak of! So what gets people downloading? The existence of SpreadFirefox.com, a Mozilla website where users post ideas for marketing schemes and volunteers put the most popular ideas into action. Its interactive website has more than 160,000 members, and Mozilla claims it has lured 10 million users away from other browsers.

Why are these mediums so successful? Because they give people the space to communicate about your products and services. Brand is not why people buy. It is the emotional attachment that they have to your brand, and it is the way that people feel about your brand that makes them purchase or not, tell a friend or not, call you to tell you all the ways you could improve or not.

This emotional attachment is generated through story telling. We are all critics and we want our opinion to be the one that is listened to. We are quick to remark to as many people as will listen about why we either loved or hated a product or service e.g. "That is the best movie I have ever seen" or "That was a total waste of money. It is not even worth getting out on DVD." When enough people agree with the story then that becomes reality. The mediums above allow the stories to spread quickly.

Advertising will not build brand equity. It is the sum of your customers' positive experiences and the stories they tell to share that experience that creates your brand equity. Having said this, a degree of marketing spend can be beneficial, provided you do some careful planning and ensure you've got a good support strategy for implementation in place. I'll share with you some of my own experiences on spending marketing dollars wisely.

chapter 12
Sensible Spending

This is a big statement from someone whose profession is advertising. He does not explicitly say that 95 percent of what we do is a waste of money, but he implies it. Knowing this, how many of you would now spend your precious marketing budgets on advertising?

I would much rather rely on good old marketing principles to guide the way I spend my budget. I need to know whose problem I am trying to solve, and tap into the knowledge that people are driven by similar aspirations of looking good, fitting in and being part of something, and that many purchases are based on emotion. I can change the media I use but the essence of a great marketing campaign remains the same, and is summed up in my so-called 'Marketing 101' – use our precious budget to do something incredulous, amazing or at least fascinating to get people talking. How outrageously memorable can we possibly be while still representing our business? People listen to word of mouth, particularly from people they trust. Get other people to spread the word about what you're doing and you'll find that you don't have to spend ridiculous amounts of money to build awareness.

It's not the size of the budget that counts, it's what you do with it that matters. We've done some pretty funny things at RedBalloon, as we know that it's OK to have fun in business. In 2003 when April 1 was approaching, we decided to do something cheeky. We designed an email campaign with some really 'out there' experiences like lava rafting, highway kayaking and learning to ride a killer whale. We loaded them as real products on the website. Each was priced at above $10,000 so we did not think that we would get many takers.

We were scheduled to send the email first thing in the morning. The Marketing Manager, who wrote it, arrived at work and announced that she had cold feet about sending it; she said, "I told my partner about it and he said that given our audience is vastly corporate he didn't think it sounded very professional." I retorted, "Who said we can't have fun in business? We don't leave our personalities at the door when we arrive at work!" So out it went.

It became our biggest single day of website traffic. People looked, laughed, and sent it on to someone else. Several people even added the products to their cart! Payment never arrived (thank goodness).

This stunt cost us almost nothing … but it was certainly PR worthy and it got people talking about us.

We've tried numerous other low-cost marketing initiatives, some which have worked and some which haven't. For instance, product placement worked for us in New Zealand, where we sponsored a prime time TV program with prizes – a huge hit. However, direct mail has not worked for us at all. But another online business that we work closely with has had great success producing millions of direct mail pieces. So when people ask me for the answer to the question, "Where should we spend our marketing dollars?" they think I'm being evasive when I say, 'It depends. There are no clear-cut answers, and what works for one does not necessarily work for someone else. What works today may not work tomorrow. Tactics may vary, but being consistent with a small budget speaks volumes.

I learned a lot about maximising a small budget while I was working for Apple. Contrary to popular belief, Apple wasn't always big. Twenty years ago, it too was trying to look bigger than it was. At Apple I learned to do a few things well, how to be noticed and how to think outside the square. In the early days Apple sometimes booked double page spreads for its ad campaigns, ran ads in prime time and did a one-off sponsorship of seat cushions at the Super Bowl, combined with a dramatic TV campaign inspired by George Orwell's '1984'. Apple did not do things like this very often, so what it did do, had to really stand out. The other thing that Apple did was to be absolutely zealous about the delivery of a consistent brand look and feel.

Jump forward a couple of decades, with vastly different technology available, and look at the different way that Apple has promoted the iPod. Initially Apple released iTunes, a software application and online music store, which gave a global community of people a tool to download and sort their music into play lists. iTunes represented the harnessing of a community defined by their collective problem, and people all over the globe caught on to the craze and flocked to buy iPods. Mainstream advertising for the iPod came later. It was not the primary vehicle for launch. This time Apple looked at the problem, solved it, and used open-source ideology to create the community, garnering the iPod's success.

Having such a small marketing budget in the early days but still achieving such rapid growth is something I am very proud of. We were thrifty when we needed to be, we tried a few things, did them well and now we are at a size where we can actually afford a real marketing budget and let me tell you, every dollar is just as precious.

LESSON LEARNED:
DO A FEW SPECTACULAR THINGS WELL
AND INVOLVE THE PEOPLE
WHO HAVE THE PROBLEM
YOU ARE TRYING TO SOLVE

chapter 13
From Good To Better

When you're doing well, when you have customers telling you they love your stuff and you've done some spectacular things to make potential customers take notice, it's very easy to think you've made it. You can now kick back and relax as the momentum of your successes will keep the business where it needs to be.

I used to think there would come a point where the website was done, the brand was established and our role was then purely to maintain it. How naïve I was. The enemy of any successful business is complacency. Thinking that you no longer need to innovate, or be responsive to changes in the consumer landscape, will overturn any company whose competitors have kept innovating and their eye sharply on the behaviours of those they serve.

I read somewhere that a Japanese philosophy is not to think in the realms of 'right or wrong' or 'good or bad' but only 'good, better'. You may very well be successful now, but it can always be 'better'. I have instilled this philosophy in the RedBalloon business to help guard against complacency. Always thinking about 'better' means that we never stop stretching our imaginations or stop dreaming of new possibilities.

We keep a close eye on potential competitors both direct and indirect, and we assess what experiences seem to be popular in other geographies. One can't assume that just because we have the biggest range that we always have the biggest craze. Sometimes you can make a discovery that surprises you. We also look at other website's features, who is launching what, what value it has, how it is solving a problem or whether it is just a gimmick. Getting complacent means dropping your guard against unexpected surprises –

you always need to be aware of who's playing in the online space. We want to change gifting forever and we are not there yet.

We keep our ear to the ground with our suppliers. Just because a certain activity is covered by insurance now, doesn't mean it will always be. Sometimes sweeping industry changes can render some activities impossible to insure to cover public liability, which happened with hang gliding a couple of years ago. Unless we speak to our suppliers regularly and ask them questions we can't find out what's going on in their many and varied industries.

Similarly with our corporate clients, it's not enough to have one meeting or to transact with them. We need to find out the challenges they face in their industries, we need to know what's topical and what issues are affecting businesses in Australia and across the Tasman.

The website is also in its sixth revision and we never run out of ways to improve it, because our customers are now driving it. They are telling us what works, what they like, what they don't, and we are listening. We want the customer experience to be at the centre of RedBalloon, whether it be for a supplier, affiliate, a purchaser or participant.

The beauty of running an internet business is the fact that the internet keeps evolving. Broadband is now more accessible than ever, 3G is next. Every advancement brings with it a plethora of new options for exciting new features.

I also need to ensure I am not complacent about my people, whose lives exist outside of the four walls of this business. This business is successful because of the people in it, who day in and day out deliver on our five core values. But if I'm not attentive to their needs and aspirations, if I

i want what she's having

don't make time to find out what drives them and what their passions are, I risk losing them to someone that will.

But complacency doesn't just impact the operational side of the business. It can also affect the emotional side and you have to ensure you don't get complacent with the vision and your overall goal. My vision is to fundamentally change gifting in Australia for ever and my BHAG of 10 per cent of the Australian and New Zealand population to experience a RedBalloon day by 2015.

Just because the numbers are currently on my side and things are moving in the right direction doesn't mean I can put this vision to the back of my mind because we are on track. The goal is 'audacious' for a reason and simply staying on track isn't going to make it. I need to continually keep my eyes open for ways to shift the business up a gear, look for new potential audiences or partnerships.

One of the main issues with being an internet-only business is that we have no shop fronts on the high street that remind people of our presence and as we are competing for the gifting dollar we need to work out how to stay front-of-mind when our potential customers are in physical retail environments.

So how can I think outside the square on this? Who can I talk to? They say the key to the race is preparation and so it is crucial that I start shaping the way things are going to go now.

THIS BUSINESS IS SUCCESSFUL
BECAUSE OF THE PEOPLE IN IT,
WHO DAY IN AND DAY OUT
DELIVER ON OUR FIVE CORE VALUES.
BUT IF I'M NOT ATTENTIVE TO
THEIR NEEDS AND
ASPIRATIONS, IF I DON'T MAKE
TIME TO FIND OUT
WHAT DRIVES THEM AND WHAT
THEIR PASSIONS ARE,
I RISK LOSING THEM TO SOMEONE
THAT WILL.

chapter 14
We Are Changing
Gifting Forever

The power of a personal thank you

I strongly believe in the power of thank you, and it is an instrumental part of my wider plan to change the nature of gifting in Australia and New Zealand forever. Creating a 'thank you' culture involves both customer and service provider – it's a two-way street. Clearly it is up to the vendor to acknowledge the customers, but I also believe that it is up to the customer to give feedback to the individual service provider. I'm sure many of us assume that it is up to the employer to recognise the contribution of their employees. But the employer is not always there to witness the employees in action. So if employees are not receiving praise or recognition from their employers then who are they receiving it from? No one … unless the customer steps in to fill this role.

Take a minute to think about who has delivered you adequate service today. The bus driver? The barista who made your coffee just the way you like it? The shoe shop assistant who arrived with endless numbers of sizes and styles for you to try? Now consider whether the simple act of their assistance was worth an acknowledgement from you? As customers we can make a big difference to how employees perceive their world, simply by acknowledging them for what is expected of them. An unexpected thank you from a customer can mean so much – it can make someone's day.

I received this email recently and I was so delighted to have made a difference.

Hi Naomi,

I heard you speak recently at Air New Zealand's leadership college at Auckland. I must confess to having never heard of you or your organisation before this. I found you a delight to listen to and lots of what you said made sense to me. I didn't really see how most of the customer contact stuff would relate to me as I work in line maintenance looking after the servicing and repair of aeroplanes before they venture off across the Pacific or Tasman. However a recent event reminded me of what you said about surprising and delighting the customer. I was onboard NZ2 for Los Angeles with 5-10 minutes to go before departure, completing some last minute stuff (refuelling, paperwork, etc) when a flight attendant asked me to check a reading light in the premium economy section. The light needed relamping so I got a spare lamp from the flight deck and replaced the failed one. After I had done this I noticed the passenger seemed really happy and he told me that in all his years of travelling he had never known an airline that would actually fix something for a passenger right before departure as I had done. This also reminded me of what you said about thanking people because being thanked in this manner made me feel fantastic for the rest of my shift and probably for a good few days after as well.

Best regards,
Shaun Houlahan

151 | i want what she's having

As customers we can really impact the level of enjoyment someone has in doing their job. I challenge you to start the ball rolling by thanking three people who assist you today; people who usually don't get noticed. The dry cleaner perhaps, or the taxi driver who got you out of the rain. If you say an authentic 'thank you' for what is expected, think about what you could do to acknowledge service that truly delights you. Would you send a handwritten note? Call their boss? Send an email to their head of public relations? In my opinion, mediocrity breeds mediocrity. As customers we have the power to determine whether an organisation delivers mediocre service or delights us. We can create an environment of acknowledgement where success breeds success.

I met a man a few years ago who has been a bus driver for 40 years, spending 33 of those years with NSW State Transit. Every day he gets his passengers to where they want to go, safely and on time. He has done this now for more than 7,000 days of his life, yet in that time he has never been acknowledged in writing by any of his customers that he has done a good job. Here is a man committed to public service, yet he has never been recognised for fulfilling this role.

What a difference, he said to me, it makes even when someone looks you in the eye, notices that you have a smile on your face, and notices that everyone arrives safely.

At 33 years something happened to Ray and he decided enough was enough. He worked out what business he was in: "It is my job to make sure that people arrive safely and on time." But Ray admitted that he had never really let his customers know that that was his job, and knew that they didn't really 'see' what he did day after day. He knew that they would notice if he did not fulfil on his job.

Ray changed his world by taking the responsibility to look each customer in the eye and say, "You can count on me to get you there on time and safely. Please enjoy the ride. It is my pleasure to be of service." He would often sing to his customers, joke and laugh, and regular customer got to know him and would share a joke. He got noticed. He had never enjoyed his job more. So after more than three decades on the job he made a choice and then in the space of only three months since making that choice, the Minister of Transport NSW received six letters acknowledging Ray for his wonderful contribution to public transport. He made a choice to take responsibility for his job and customers took the time to notice.

What a difference each of us can make simply by noticing what we take for granted. Each of us has the power to spur people to greatness. I don't mean that we should pander to mediocrity. But if people do the job, add value or make a contribution, simply say thank you and help spur them on to greater things. Life is not about what you can get but what you can give to others.

As you know I love to be on the phones at work, making myself a Pleasure Relations consultant on a regular basis. I spoke to a customer some months ago who said in a gruff voice, "I want to speak to somebody responsible." I thought, "Oh I guess that would be me", inside dreading that this was going to be a bad call. He continued, "I was given one of YOUR experiences as a retirement gift from my company and quite frankly I was not happy. I found myself driving to the experience and I was uncomfortable, in fact so uncomfortable that I decided to turn the car around and go home." I wondered what would make him so uncomfortable that he could not keep going.

He continued, "Then I realised that what I was experiencing was something I had not felt since I was a four year old going to a birthday party. I was excited. Ever since I was a little boy I had wanted to fly an airplane, and now I had been given a hands-on training flight. I had to talk to myself and say, 'This is silly, do I really not like these planes that much?' So I turned the car around and after my briefing session, I got to take off, fly and land an air craft. I don't know why in my 65 years I had never got around to it, but I wanted to say thank you to someone who was responsible." I humbly said, "It was my pleasure."

When we started RedBalloon, I had no idea how much of a difference we were going to make to people, giving people the opportunity to do things they always wanted to do. I had created a vision, but the impact of that vision was totally unimaginable.

Creating a culture of thank you, is just a small part of my plan to change gifting in Australia and New Zealand forever. I challenge you to thank three people authentically today and for the next 21 days. Look them in the eye and notice, acknowledge and recognise the contribution they've made. It must be real and come from the heart. After 21 days it should hopefully become a habit. If we all do this, imagine what a difference we can make not just to individuals but to the economy.

"If it's meant to be, it's up to me!" From John Hunter, Director of ONE Group

I love what I do. I love knowing how many people get to have a good time as a result of what we do. I love watching my team learn, grow and develop. I love to know that we are reminding people about the art of gifting and reinforcing that a great gift shows just how much people care.

When I was a child my mother taught me the art of gifting and also about being a gracious recipient. I had not realised that, like Sunday roasts, this was something that was culturally being lost. I'm really determined to remind people of the importance of gifting, whether it be for personal or corporate purposes. Gifting is a demonstration of our love for one another. It shows leadership, friendship, connectedness, and commitment.

> "The fragrance always stays in the hand that gives the rose."
> Shakespeare

Gifting is not just about the gift itself. It is also the intent of the gift which counts. Have you ever received a gift that you know is recycled? You know that it has been somewhere else before and it doesn't make you feel particularly special. Or you know that you got the last gift in the gift cupboard because the gift has no relevance to you at all.

I gave a friend of mine a baby lullaby machine on the occasion of the birth of her first son. The machine was supposed to play sweet music when the baby awoke to coax it back to sleep. When my daughter was born, back came the baby lullaby machine to me, wrapped up with a special note; "This is what you gave us. We got a 'sleeper' so we never needed this gift. We hope it works as well for you." I got a sleeper, too. So for her next child, back went the lullaby machine. But she got another sleeper and so still did not need the gift. When I had my second child, the same scenario repeated itself. By this time, we had jokingly made up a story that if you were given the lullaby machine then you would get a sleeper, which of course is the greatest gift you can give any new parent!

On the assumption that my friend would have no more children we both agreed to give the gift to another new mum that we both knew, to pass on the magic of getting a sleeper. I think we even left the cards inside from the previous times it had been gifted. Unfortunately our friend was less than impressed with the lullaby machine which was clearly not a first hand gift. Even when we shared so delightedly our experiences about how wonderful this gift had been for both of us, she didn't buy the story at all about it being magical. She did not get a sleeper and the magic of the gift was lost.

The greatest lesson I learned from this experience was that it's not just about the gift itself; it is the thought, emotion and intent behind the gift that matters the most. Gifting is an extension of us, and demonstrates our connection to others, and we literally have the power to give a piece of magic to people we love, care for or want to make a difference to.

Spontaneous and unexpected gifts often delight even more than those that are somehow expected. My wonderful husband will often buy me a gift when he sees something he knows that I will absolutely love. But sometimes for Christmas or birthdays he is a bit challenged finding gifts that I would truly love. I'd rather he showed his love when he sees something just right for me. Sometimes he has been very cunning and underhand to find exactly what he knows I would like. I once saw something I liked in a shop in Singapore and unbeknownst to me he arranged for a friend to buy it and bring it back to Australia in time for Christmas. I was truly surprised and delighted.

A friend of mine knows that her partner loves Rugby. Some years ago, the Sydney CBD was adorned with flags to celebrate the World Cup. She contacted the city council after the event and arranged to get one of the flags for her partner. He was so delighted and it was the perfect gift for him. It was not the price of the gift that mattered; it was that it was something he really appreciated and he knew the effort that his partner had gone to.

"From booking our yacht B&B experience to actually 'living' it, I couldn't have dreamed of a better and more indulgent way of proposing to my girlfriend Vanessa. Aided by perfect weather and an extremely helpful and friendly crew we spent an afternoon sailing the Sydney Harbour, only to return back to base to upgrade to a larger, more luxurious yacht for our B&B overnight stay. Pampered by a masseuse for an hour, we were then left alone to enjoy a remarkable seafood banquet. Later in the evening, whilst sipping champagne and watching the sun set over the city skyline, I knew I couldn't have found a more romantic setting and I found the right words to propose. I am happy to say that a tearful and happy YES was returned. We awoke in the morning to tranquil, calm waters and watched for an hour the world

157 | i want what she's having

wake up around us. Eventually the skipper returned to lead us back to shore and a delicious breakfast at a cafe in Darling Harbour. It was a weekend I will never forget and one Vanessa and I will tell our children! Thank you RedBalloon for making our dream come true!!" Craig Saundry

A spontaneous gift or a simple thank you can make someone's day. Remind yourself of the delight of personal gifting by surprising someone with an unexpected gesture and I guarantee you'll get a feel for what it is that I am 'on' every day.

Thanking in the Corporate Sphere

In one of many emails that I subscribe to, I was faced with a question that really struck a chord with me: "Do you want loyal customers or committed employees?" My answer was, without a doubt, committed employees. Committed and engaged employees will look after my customers, turning them into happy, loyal customers, which will in turn boost profits. This can be summed up in a simple formula:

Happy People + Happy Customers = Happy Profits

In fact we put together the evidence for this in our corporate book *The Little Red Book of Answers*. There is such an incredible amount of research on the benefits of having an engaged workforce and on how to attract great people to work at your organisation.

Business is simple. There are two ways to make a business profitable – you either sell more or you reduce costs. If you get a bill for something, you analyse it and establish if there are any savings that can be made. But there is no monthly bill to let us know what disengaged employees have cost us that month. What does it cost a business when the employees are daydreaming, wishing they were somewhere else, gossiping or just not showing up? The Gallup Organisation, which conducts global surveys on employee engagement has the numbers for 2006.

Disengaged employees cost Australian businesses around AUS $32.7 billion per annum
Disengaged employees cost New Zealand businesses around NZ$3.7 billion per annum

Engaged Employees are those who work with passion and feel a profound connection to their company. They drive innovation and move the organisation forward and unfortunately only 21 per cent of Australian workers are like this (25 per cent of New Zealanders).

Not-Engaged Employees are those that are essentially 'checked-out'. They're sleepwalking through their workday, putting time but not energy or passion into their work. 61 per cent of Australians and 64 per cent of New Zealanders are not engaged.

Actively Disengaged Employees are those that aren't just unhappy at work, they're busy acting out their unhappiness. Every day these workers undermine what their engaged co-workers accomplish. 18 per cent of Australians and 11 per cent of New Zealanders are actively disengaged.

i want what she's having

From the above figures it's clear that Australian employees are less engaged than New Zealanders. Furthermore, this study also revealed that Australian employees are the second least engaged in the world after the French. What a frightening piece of information, and you can imagine what sort of impact this is having on our economy.

Employees who are thinking that the grass is greener somewhere else are simply not productive. How can they be loving your customers and really giving them an experience that delights them if they are busy thinking what a terrible organisation it is that they are working for? Customers pick up on the lack of authenticity.

Our workforce has so much work to do to improve the levels of disengagement and I'm committed to driving this change in whatever small way I can to at least get the ball rolling, supported by my RedBalloon team. RedBalloon is striving to increase employee engagement by reminding companies of the importance of recognition and acknowledgement through gifting and that it is OK to have fun in success.

Where to start though? A good initial question to ask yourself is would your staff advocate your business as a great place to work? Only 3 per cent of employees who are not engaged with an organisation will recommend it as a great place to work, while 67 per cent of engaged people will tell people what a great employer they have (Gallup Organisation 2006). It's never too late to take steps to make an organisation into one that people want to work for and to become an 'Employer of Choice'. I was inspired by the tiny book *FISH – A Remarkable Way to Boost Morale and Improve Results* by Stephen C. Lundin, Harry Paul and John Christensen, and I encourage you to seek out a copy and share it.

Secondly, ask yourself how many employees does your company have? This is the number of people either playing for your team and openly promoting you, or worse – being silent. Remember that employees are customers too. What are they saying about the product or the company itself, and are they saying anything at all? If your employees are disengaged, only 13 per cent will recommend their employers' products or services, while a massive 78 per cent of engaged employees will tell anyone and everyone about their brand and products, because they love being a part of something great.

As a case in point, I recruited a new team member some time ago, and she received her official job offer on a Friday. I got an email on the Monday from her to say, "If I could possibly have my business cards now that would be great. I must have told 70 people on the weekend about this amazing company I am going to work for, and it would really have helped to have a business card to make sure they got the name right and to remind them to look us up." Her immediate engagement with the company was astounding and her actions (raving to 70 other people about how amazing her organisation is) are such great publicity for the

i want what she's having

company! Naturally one would hope that new employees are excited to be joining an organisation, but it is then up to the company to keep them interested and engaged.

There is a popular theory that people resign from bad managers, not bad companies. More than 44 per cent of Australian employees say the poor quality of their managers makes them very unhappy at work. Engineering tops the list of the unhappiest industry in which to work, according to Seek's 2006 survey of Employee Satisfaction and Motivation. However, the good news is that workers are overall much happier this year than they were last year. 37 per cent say they are happy or very happy compared with 21 per cent in the same categories last year.

Top 5 Happy Industries;
Community and Sports – 51 percent
Science and Technology – 49 percent
HR and Recruitment – 48 percent
Consulting/Corporate Strategy – 44 percent
Construction – 43 percent

People don't hang around if they don't feel valued, particularly in a tight labour market where people have choices. The labour market has moved from a model that values security to a model that prizes personal fulfilment. The challenge facing companies now is how to make the week as rewarding as the weekend, as this is what employees are looking for.

The biggest cost of having disengaged employees is not just the cost of rehiring people to replace the ones who leave. It's the hidden costs of lost knowledge and relationships that cause severe blows to the organisation. Organisations with a low level of employee engagement face a continual treadmill of attracting talent, training them up, trying to engage them unsuccessfully and then watching them walk out the door before the whole process begins again, each time with the hope that 'this time it might be different'. It is a vicious cycle. To break out of it the company must look for the common element in each of the scenarios and work to improve or change that element.

I remember one of my fellow entrepreneurs bemoaning that he had had 22 sales people in the past 2 years and that only one of them had worked out. "Sales people are impossible to recruit," he said. I asked him, "What was the one consistent element in all those relationships?" "Well I recruited them all," he said, "but sales people know how to sell themselves." "So you're the constant element in all of those relationships?" I asked. He was not pleased by my observation. By nature we seem to avoid responsibility. As the business owner, manager or HR person in charge of recruitment, it is up to us to take responsibility for asking that question. I am responsible for who I recruit, how they

i want what she's having

perform and how they are led. If I have a history of not being good at it, I must stop doing that job and get someone else who can recruit, manage and lead to do it.

I continually ask myself the question, "How do I match up?" Do we practise what we preach at RedBalloon? I find working in a business with 40 people much more intimate than working in a big organisation, as you have the chance to really get to know what rocks peoples' boats. I have learned that every single person is completely different and it's important to understand why people work and what they want from a job.

I heard Reg Athwal speak about recruiting great talent. He argued that knowing why people work was essential. He used the acronym F.O.R.M. for it:

FAMILY/FRIENDS – People work for the reason of family and friends, not just necessarily to support them, but to be near them. They need to do something that they think is important.

OCCUPATION – For the betterment of their occupation. What can they learn that is new, what is the social acceptance of the role, what is the next step in their ultimate goal? These people are on a mission.

RECREATION – Recreation is important to this group. Work is a means to an end. They are tennis players, cooks, artists, charity volunteers. They work to support their 'habit' (or hobby, but it is more than just a hobby, it is a passion). This is where they get their purpose.

MONEY – Then there are those who work for the money and money alone. According to Reg these are the ones who will take the next best offer that comes along. So they are unlikely to be loyal in any way.

For me it's about valuing the contribution of each person and ensuring that they get noticed. People need to have a sense of related validation – 'I feel great about what I do, I make a difference and others know about it'. It's very important to have a shared experience of achievement.

"The most consistently profitable divisions have people doing what they like to do, with people they like, with a strong sense of psychological ownership for the outcome of their work." Coffman C & Harter J, (1999). A Hard Look at Soft Numbers. The Gallup Organisation.

Marcus Buckingham and Curt Coffman in *First Break all the Rules* argue that it's not just about having great people, they must be in the right roles and well managed. They also affirm the important role of acknowledgement and recognition in employee engagement.

Recognition and Reward

Many people leave a job simply because they are not recognised. Recognising employees for their expected and unexpected contributions is a vital ingredient in attracting and retaining a fabulous team. It's important though to separate the difference between recognition and reward.

Recognition is about noticing someone and letting them know that I noticed in a heartfelt and authentic way. Recognition in the corporate sphere is no different to that of the personal or public sphere, and I'm so passionate

165 |

about spreading the power of thank you and encouraging acknowledgement amongst all groups in society.

A reward is a gift that demonstrates recognition. It is not an incentive, i.e. if you do this you will get that. Rewards are often unexpected and are designed to delight and inspire the recipient, and affirm their behaviour. Corporate rewards or gifts are no different to personal gifts and carry the same significance of intent. Corporate gifting is an extension of the organisation and the brand, and must demonstrate the values of the giver. It must also strengthen the relationship with the receiver.

RedBalloon's vision to change gifting in Australia and New Zealand forever involves encouraging companies to put in place formal systems for recognising and rewarding staff through gifting.

"The bottom line is that people make great companies: the innovativeness, values, energy and alignment of our people are the forces that make us great. Any failure on our part to utilise the unique capabilities and strengths of diversity is lost opportunity of immense proportion. It is born inertia. We should cut through the tradition and rhetoric of our current paradigm and create a very different type of organisation... We must take the risk, because there is none. It will be worth it," John McFarlane – CEO, ANZ 2004

At RedBalloon we have worked with hundreds of organisations that are really committed to their people. I recently commented to one of the consultants at the Gallup

Organisation, "Don't you think that this is all done and dusted? Everyone has read the right books, seen the research results and knows that it is 'people first'?" My somewhat biased view is that organisations do love their people. Being the CEO of RedBalloon which has a very extensive Corporate program providing reward and recognition programs for hundreds of companies, means that I get to deal with organisations who have already worked this out and are already acknowledging their staff. But apparently I have a skewed view of the world as there are thousands of other organisations, big and small, that we are not having conversations with, who still believe that employees are dispensable. Or worse still, they endure their staff until they make enough profit to run their business without people. You cannot fake it 'til you make it – you either honour your employees or you don't.

The organisations that love their people use some form of employee reward and recognition program. Why do you need an official program to recognise your employees? Quite simply because people forget. We all get busy and unless it is really a habit most team leaders forget to notice the contribution of their team members. According to Marcus Buckingham in *First Break All The Rules* it can take as little as seven days for people to forget that they were praised for doing good work.

Over the past five years, we've assisted many companies to set up and maintain such programs, and we have discovered that there seem to be three key elements to a successful reward program:

1. Acknowledgement – How do employees want to be noticed and acknowledged?

i want what she's having

2. Do they get to choose what to do?
3. Does the reward give the employee a sense of achievement?

But above all, a reward and recognition program must have integrity. It must not be there just for show. The managers or people in charge of executing the employee recognition program must be behind it 100 percent and believe in its value.

Marcus Buckingham & Curt Coffman in First Break All the Rules acknowledge that "… if your relationship with your manager is fractured, then no amount of in-chair massaging or company-sponsored dog walking will persuade you to stay and perform. It is better to work for a great manager in an old-fashioned company than for a terrible manager in a company offering an enlightened, employee-focused culture."

Employees will see through a program that has no substance. It will not work to enthuse and motivate staff and could even contribute to disengagement.

We also believe in incorporating an element of fun into a reward and recognition program. According to Mr Weinstein of Playfair Inc, "The difficulty with a standardised reward and recognition program is that it is a completely impersonal process. Instead of thinking about the specific people involved, the company provides the same process and generic rewards to everyone. But when an element of fun and play is added ... the experience becomes personalised and much more memorable for the award recipient. Without any additional expenditure, the reward can become even more meaningful." The sheer variety of RedBalloon experiences provide plenty of opportunities for fun and play to be incorporated into a company's reward program.

As Mr Weinstein mentions, an element of personalisation is important in a recognition program. Generic rewards simply don't appeal to the entire workplace. Some months ago a client shared with me the following story of a woman he knew who had been a team leader and then promoted to head up a small call centre of fifty people. She said to herself, "I am going to really show my people that I care." There was one exceptional 'star' performer in her team and she wanted to make sure he was acknowledged and that his colleagues knew what a contribution he made. She arranged an awards dinner and invited the star team member to come and accept his beautifully framed award certificate. However what she got was anything other than glee. In fact under his breath, though loud enough for people to hear, he made a derogatory remark about what the company could do with its plaque. The new manager was extremely embarrassed.

Over the following 12 months this star employee continued to be an outstanding performer. The new manager really wanted to let him know that he was noticed and appreciated but did not want to go through the humiliation of another awards ceremony. Passing by his desk one day she noticed some photos of his kids throughout his workstation. She spoke to his colleagues and found out that the most important things in his life were his children.

The manager contacted the star employee's wife and secretly arranged to have a professional photo shoot of his children. They were sworn to secrecy and the wife and children ended up having a fantastic day.

The awards dinner came around again and this time when the star performer's name was read out, he rolled his eyes as all he could see as he came to the podium was the reverse of the frame. When the frame was turned around his eyes filled with tears as he beheld his beautiful children. The only response he could manage was to whisper his thanks and mouth how beautiful the award was.

And of course when he got home his children were so excited to share their side of the story that they had kept a secret. They also understood the significance of the special award that their dad had received. This man did the job he did because of the flexible hours so he could be with his children after school. Make rewards personal and don't be afraid to be creative and inject a sense of fun.

If a third of people are currently looking for a job elsewhere, I'm confident that a big difference can be made just by acknowledging people in a meaningful way for what they contribute. If we as customers, not just as employers, acknowledge people we can change these disastrous employee engagement figures.

The dilemma of choice

Roughly a year ago, I delivered a presentation on the three elements of a successful rewards program at a breakfast for business leaders. Afterwards, I was taken aside by one of the attendees who said to me, "You were saying that people will share their experiences much more than they will talk about their possessions. Well I agree to a point, but not all experiences are worth talking about."

I asked her to clarify what she meant because all the research that I have read says that an organisation using experiential rewards can spend as little as half the amount to get the same result as a program based on cash or merchandise. This theory is based on the knowledge that people want to share their awards with family or friends.

From our very own RedBalloon survey research in 2005, we confirmed this theory. We asked 'How do you want to be rewarded for a job well done?', and only 1 percent said with a desk accessory, 4 percent said with flowers, 1.4 percent said with a CD/DVD voucher and 1.7 percent with movie tickets. 17 percent said they'd like a dinner out although these are really hard to organise and can be embarrassing at expense claim time. 56 percent of survey respondents said a fun activity with family and friends was their reward of choice.

Knowing this, I was quite surprised at this woman's statement. She explained further that she had a job putting on events, and what her manager did to thank her was arrange to have some personal items delivered to the suite of a hotel and this woman got to spend the weekend at the hotel. She said that this 'experience' was the loneliest weekend of her life. As a single mother she simply hated being a canary in a gilded cage. I responded, "From what you have heard in my presentation, what was the element that was missing in this sort of reward?" After some thought she realised that it was choice. There was no consideration for how she'd like to be rewarded and what would be special to her.

Even now after putting together countless reward programs for other companies, we still never assume that we will know which experience someone will choose. You never know what they have always wanted to get up to, try, challenge themselves with or do again for fun. So we offer over 1,000 experiences to give people choice. And we will never stop adding to the range.

Ask yourself this question: 'I have always wanted to ... ?' Now aren't you likely to tell others when you finally achieve it? It is the sense of achievement that puts people on top of the world. I feel fantastic when I've done something to be proud of, something that was not necessarily easy but I worked at it and got a result. People want to be able to tell the world what a great thing they've done, but culturally we don't tend to big-note ourselves so we don't tend to tell people of our successes. But if you get to say, "Oh I got to take off, fly and land a helicopter," people will instantly ask, "Really, how come?" And it's a great way to start a conversation about your achievement and how you were rewarded. Experiences give people the chance to live out their achievements, creating memories in the process, reminding them of the fabulous thing they've achieved, and hopefully encouraging similar behaviour in their next task or project.

In some of the more successful reward and recognition programs I have seen, companies have produced a 'Hero Board' where people come and stick photos of themselves doing their RedBalloon experiences. Another client has a Friday afternoon 'Home movie' drinks session where staff bring a DVD or digital photos of their experience to share with the group, and everyone loves to imagine what they will do when it's their turn for a RedBalloon Day.

> "The future depends on what we do in the present."
> Mahatma Gandhi

It could be considered odd that my background as a marketer renders me so passionate about the people element of organisations. The thing is, I have seen so many fantastic promotional campaigns die a slow death because the people within the organisation just did not get behind it. Despite Nike's large spend on advertising, the in-store experience just does not meet the expectations raised by the advertising, and Nike's turnover has suffered as a result. Without the support of an engaged team who deliver a consistent experience for the customer, consumers become increasingly cynical to advertising, and then ultimately cynical to the brand. Having your employees engaged with the business is critical to the authenticity of any campaign.

The results for companies who authentically acknowledge the critical role that their employees play speak for themselves. Jim Collins clearly shows in his research for his book *Good to Great* the difference in businesses that get great people, retain great people and have a culture of CEOs being promoted from within rather than being hired externally.

> "Stock prices of companies with high morale outperformed similar companies in the same industries by more than two to one in 2004. The research found that companies with low morale lagged behind their industry competitors by almost five to one. The global study focused on 28 publicly traded companies with a total of more than 920,000 employees."

i want what she's having

"Stock prices of these companies were compared to the industry average for more than 6,000 other companies in the same industries. It found that high-morale companies provide the three main things that matter most to employees: fair treatment; a sense of achievement in their work and pride in their employer; and good, productive relationships with other employees."
High morale accompanies high stock. (2004) Sirota Consulting LLC, www.sirota.com

That is why our simple equation **happy people + happy customers = happy profits** has been so pivotal in our focus.

RedBalloon In Mid-Flight
Some Final Thoughts

I get asked regularly, "What is the one single thing that you did to make your business successful?" Great question, but it has no answer. It is not that I have no comment on the subject; this whole book has been full of my comments! But if it was one single thing, don't you think that everybody else would be doing exactly the same? Furthermore, by definition, these businesses would not be successful because every business would be doing the same thing.

What creates the concept of success is that it has a reference point. You can only say you are successful if you have something to compare yourself against. It is why we love the BRW lists: fastest growing privately held business, Upstarts, Fast 100, Top 500, top female entrepreneurs, top young entrepreneurs, best exporter ... the list of lists is endless. It's also why we love an award. Success is about comparing how one business is faring against another. But is our success as businesses only to be measured in profits? What about the innovation, the jobs created, the building of something that will last, or creating a better world – how do we judge those?

For me success really comes down to what it is that you set out to do and how you played the game to achieve it.

Who wrote the book on success anyway? Imagine if Martians came to earth and saw a game of soccer being played. They have no idea about the rules or why it is that when a net stops a round object people cheer really loudly and hug each other. Quite frankly it makes no sense at all. They might guess at the rules and see that there are two competing teams but still it makes absolutely no sense because they do not understand that there is a score.

Scorecards tell us whether we are on track to win the game or not and business is also just a game. One of my dear friends often reminds me if I am getting very serious about something: "Did anybody get hurt today because of this disaster?" "No." "Ah, so you've just lost sight of the fact that you are playing the business game?" "Yes."

According to Verne Harnish in *Mastering the Rockafeller Habits* there are three success factors for a fast growing business:

1. A clearly articulated vision
2. Know the numbers/metrics that drive success
3. Have a communication 'rhythm'

I believe that knowing this is one thing, but delivering upon it is something completely different.

I'm still constantly learning about what will sell. I sometimes say, "We can't sell that, that's shocking," and it sells like hotcakes, so clearly I'm not an expert. I am great for knowing what would appeal to a forty year-old woman but we sell to anyone aged eight to eighty and you've got to have an absolute range, which is why we have everything from belly-dancing to bread making to ballooning to barista courses. We must appeal to the whole community to meet our own BHAG.

RedBalloon is on a wonderful journey, with so much potential, many goals to accomplish and many adventures yet to have. I've learnt so much on my life's journey so far and continue to be challenged, delighted and amazed every day.

Marketing is about continually listening to your customer and discovering what they heard, learned, liked and loved.

i want what she's having

What were they delighted by? Then you fine-tune the product, service or customer experience, learn more and then fine tune again, every time making sure that the marketing message is authentic, real and related to the customers it set out to engage.

The future for me is not about revenue. Of course, a business must be profitable to keep investing. My main focus is about orchestrating change – it's about what I can give.

If I can change the way people give, to transform the concept of gifts from useless, poorly thought-out token items to something of value and experience, I have made a difference in the lives of both the giver and the receiver. If I can move employee engagement by just one percent by helping corporations treat their staff and make them feel valued, thus finding greater satisfaction in their work and meaning in life in general, I have made a difference.

I love what I do. I love knowing how many people get to have a good time as a result of what we do. I love watching my team learn, grow and develop. I love to know that we have helped people rediscover the art of gifting and that a great gift shows just how much people care. I'm really determined to remind people of the importance of gifting, whether it be personal or corporate.

I want RedBalloon to be responsible for changing the nature of gifting in Australia and New Zealand, to the point that everyone in these two countries has had a RedBalloon Day. Then imagine it, when people see a red balloon, it will remind them of that one day when they were given a wonderful gift, a beautiful memory, the perfect experience.

I never tire of hearing customer stories. A customer, David Boyce bought his father a DC3 flight for his 84th birthday. He said his dad had always loved planes, always talked about planes and so he arranged it as a surprise. Being driven down to Sydney from the Central Coast, David's father had no idea where he was going.

"He was 'over the moon' when he realised this was his birthday present. My partner and I decided to accompany him on the flight and it will be one of the best memories I have shared with my father. He hasn't stopped talking about flying low at 500ft along the northern beaches and taking in the beautiful coastline, the smooth ride and the friendly staff. I recommend this experience to young and old. Thank you RedBalloon." David Boyce

We are clearly creating the future and it is exciting to be shaping the way in which people 'give' – forever.

The future direction of RedBalloon will come from internally and from externally – from the feedback our customers give us and by us not resting on our laurels.

After all my years in business I have realised that advertising is a waste of time – it's absolutely hollow – unless you have a great team around you. So a big thank you must go to my team – current, future, and past, who are the ones with the passion, purpose and commitment to change gifting in the region forever.

Thank you also to all those who gave us a go, to the supply partners who said 'yes', the people who regularly visit the site to see what is new, those who share their gifting challenges with us, and to the mentors and business people who generously share what they have learned.

i want what she's having

Five years down the track with the privilege of hindsight – would I do it again? Some days 'yes' and others 'no'. Starting and running a business is an adventure-filled journey, with many highs and lows, so I guess it depends on when you ask me this question! But I think I'm focused enough on my vision and what we are working to achieve not to be distracted by thoughts of 'should I' or 'shouldn't I'. I'm committed to our BHAG and I'm excited about the possibilities ahead (there are still too many people to delight with our RedBalloon experiences!) so I'm enjoying the RedBalloon ride.

Now you know exactly what I'm on!

Brilliant business books

Although there are many brilliant business books out there, here is a small selection that I constantly refer to:

Malcom Gladwell *The Tipping Point*
Jim Collins *Built to Last*
Jim Collins *Good to Great*
Seth Godden *Purple Cow*
Seth Godden *All Marketers are Liars*
Verne Harnish *Mastering the Rockefeller Habits*
Stephen C. Lundin, Harry Paul and John Christensen *Fish – A Remarkable Way to Boost Morale and Improve Results*
Marcus Buckingham & Curt Coffman *First Break all the Rules*
Robert E. Kaplan *Know your Strengths*
Ike Bain *The Dick Smith Way*
Ken Blanchard and Barbara Glanz *The Simple Truths of Service – Inspired by Johnny the Bagger*
Michael Feiner *The Feiner Points of Leadership*

Visit www.naomisimson.com.au to continue to follow the RedBalloon journey.

i want what she's having

Naomi Simson

Naomi Simson is passionate about pleasure! So much so she created a business based on fun. As the founder and Chief Experiences Officer (CEO) of RedBalloon Days Naomi is passionate about helping others to find their own source of happiness and pleasure. Given that the average life has 27,615 days she wonders how many of these are truly memorable and how she can make sure they are.

Driven by a seemingly endless source of enthusiasm and energy, Naomi has a big vision to change gifting forever in Australia and New Zealand. RedBalloon has been nothing short of an online phenomena fueled by Naomi's desire to offer amazing gifts to excite and inspire.

For Naomi life is a journey in the search of answers, one to be celebrated and shared. Passionate about sharing her wealth of experience and knowledge, Naomi is a regular on the speaking circuit and writes a blog to help others reach their own personal and professional goals.

Naomi's background is in corporate marketing at IBM, KPMG, Apple Computer Australia and Ansett Australia. In 2005 she was recognised as Westpac NSW Entrepreneur of the Year. No stranger to breaking new ground or going it alone, in 2006 Naomi was the only female on BRW's Fastest Growing Start Ups list.

Amidst juggling her commitments as CEO of RedBalloon she is also the President of Sydney chapter of the Entrepreneurs Organisation (2007–08) and a mother of two. She lives in Balmain, Sydney, with her wonderful husband Peter, their fantastic kids Natalia and Oscar, and their companion canine Dexter.

Read daily updates about Naomi's business concepts, findings and insights on her blog at www.naomisimson.com.au